Best of
HEALTHY EXCHANGES ®
FOOD NEWSLETTER '92

Common Sense Ways of
Fat and Sugar Modification
in Uncommonly Good Ways. ™

by
JoAnna M. Lund

First Edition 1993

Art layout by
Rebecca Dierickx Pelletier & Judy McNamara

DEDICATION

This book is dedicated to everyone who has made my dream of creating "common people" healthy recipes a reality.

First, to the great men and women in the media who helped me get my common sense message of cooking and living out to the general public.

To all the wonderful people I've met through sharing my recipes, and asking me to write another cookbook because they just couldn't get enough of my recipes.

To Shirley, for typing, retyping and then typing the recipes again. She learned early on I can't spell.

To Rose, for coming along just when I needed help computing the diabetic exchanges. She's a true professional with a "down to earth" approach to health.

To Ruth, Betty, Gayle, Barb, Juanita, Phyllis, Beth, Kris, Sandy, Lisa, Jaime and Loretta for helping me physically get the newsletters ready for the post office. Yes, we have both fun and a HEALTHY EXCHANGES buffet when we are done each month, but it still is a lot of work folding and labeling the newsletters.

To Nancy and Dave, for helping me verbalize my dreams and saying "Gee Whiz, why not?"

To Mary Ann, Cindy, Trish, Judy and Tom for setting up, printing and compiling the newsletter and this cookbook. The dream would have stopped before it started if they didn't give it 'their all' each month.

And, last but not least, to my family. To my sisters, Mary and Regina and their families, for being staunch cheerleaders all the way. To my children, Tom, James and Pam, Becky and Matt for saying "that a way, Mom!" To my newest taster, grandson Zach. His smile while sampling the food is the highlight of my day. And, especially to my husband and official taste tester, Cliff. Without his physical and moral support none of this could have happened. My family didn't squash my dream of sharing healthy recipes, but rather helped me realize it and dream even larger than I first envisioned.

Forward

I have been delighted and inspired in my work with JoAnna Lund and Healthy Exchanges. It is wonderful to have such a tried and true resource for my patients who are working to manage diabetes and heart disease or simply trying to change to a healthy diet. They can be confident that these recipes are acceptable and workable in their meal plans and always high in flavor. The best part, of course, is that they are such "normal" foods that anyone would want to eat them.

"Pie in the sky!" Well, it seems that cooking the low fat, low sugar way has reached new limits and we can all thank Healthy Exchanges for giving many of us a helping hand.

Rose Hoenig, RD

ABOUT THE DIETITIAN AND AUTHOR

Rose Hoenig, RD,LD is a licensed, registered dietitian practicing in the Quad Cities. She is a graduate of Marycrest College, Davenport, IA and a member of the American Dietetic Association, Iowa Dietetic Association and President Elect of the Mississippi Valley Dietetic Association. She is also a member of the Iowa Consulting Dietitians in Health Care Facilities. Rose provides nutrition counseling to physicians and for various health care facilities. She and her husband Tony, live in Bettendorf, IA and have three children, Doug, Dan and Becky.

JoAnna Lund made a mid life career change from Commercial Insurance Underwriter to recipe developer when she was handed a burden she could not solve with cake donuts (three children involved in the Persian Gulf War). The day she took her son to the Quad Cities Airport to leave for Saudi, she drove him there with 56 inch hips. JoAnna was a professional dieter for almost 30 years, so she knew what she was not going to do. She was not going to diet, but rather find a workable solution both she and her trucker husband could live with. Her goal was to only get healthy so she would not be an added burden to the family. JoAnna is a graduate of the University of Western Illinois, a member of the International Association of Culinary Professionals and a member of the Mid America Publishers Association. JoAnna and her husband Cliff, live in DeWitt, IA. They are the parents of three children, Becky Pelletier, James, and Tom Dierickx, and have two wonderful children-in-law, Matt, husband of Becky and Pam, wife of James. In addition, the newest member of the family is their grandson Zachary, son of James and Pam.

TABLE OF CONTENTS

INTRODUCTION

New Year's Day, 1992, while my trucker husband Cliff was "on the road again", I assembled the first 207 newsletters in my living room. These were for people who in blind faith, signed up as charter subscribers. They didn't know what they would be getting, but knew I would continue to share the types of recipes I created for my first cookbook. They told me their families liked the food they cooked from my recipes and wanted more. As I write this, about 18 months later, the number is well over 12,000.

Why did my dream grow like this? Well, I like to think it is because these recipes are for "common people" who want to eat healthier, but for personal reasons of their own, do not want to use recipes that call for ingredients found only in health food stores or use complicated cooking procedures.

The guidelines I use for any recipe I create or share with others still follow the same ones I set for myself when I "threw together" my first recipe many months ago. They are (1) low in fat, sugar and reasonably low in sodium (2) easy to prepare. I still say "if it takes longer to fix it than to eat it, forget it!" (3) the portion must be tasty, satisfying and have eye appeal (4) all ingredients must be found in the neighborhood grocery.

By creating recipes based on these guidelines, I've gone on to lose 130 pounds and my husband, Cliff over 30 pounds. We did not sacrifice flavor, but rather only gave up the excess fats and sugars.

The idea for this cookbook was born when I started receiving so many notes and letters from subscribers who signed up after the first year, telling me, "I just didn't believe I'd get this many recipes each month. Can I get the back issues?" or "Thank you for sharing recipes the whole family will sit and eat together. I'd like the back issues. Are they still available?" Well, as the HEALTHY EXCHANGES FOOD NEWSLETTER took another "pioneering step" January 1993, by including 3 separate ways to calculate the recipes (1) weight loss exchanges (2) calories with fat grams, etc. and (3) diabetic specific exchanges, I decided to calculate the "reader's favorites" from the 1992 editions based on this additional data and feature these in this cookbook.

I chose to add this nutrient information when I realized how many diabetics and heart patients were using my recipes, in addition to those using them to lose weight. We all have different reasons for wanting to eat healthy, but the bottom line still has to be tasty food in realistic portions.

One of the hardest tasks was determining which recipes to include. So, I asked the subscribers to let me know what recipes became family favorites for them. The response was wonderful. I then took the "unofficial" poll winners and these are the featured recipes. I hope you enjoy these recipes as much as the subscribers have. Welcome to the Healthy Exchanges Family. Remember, **It's Not a Diet, It's a Way of Life.**

Joanna,
Cliff and
Grandson Zachary

HEALTHY EXCHANGES
STANDARD RECIPE LEGEND

The Diabetic Specific Exchanges are calculated by a Registered Dietitian and the other calculations are computer based.

The following symbols are used after each recipe.

SM = Milk	Ve = Vegetable
Fa = Fat	Pr = Protein
Br = Bread	Fr = Fruit
Sl = Slider	OC = Optional Calories
St = Starch	Mt = Meat
Ca = Carbohydrate	So = Sodium

These symbols will be used for all Weight Loss Exchanges (HEALTHY EXCHANGES); Grams (gr); Diabetic Specific Exchanges listed .

**For additional information about
HEALTHY EXCHANGES/Weight Loss Exchanges,**
refer to pages **7** through **13** in this book
for extensive explanation.

*Should you need additional information,
please feel free to call*
319-659-8234

HEALTHY EXCHANGES WEIGHT LOSS EXCHANGES

Most of you using this book are already familiar with food exchanges. You can skip this part and begin using and enjoying the recipes, counting them towards your daily totals.

And for those of you who want to use the recipes because they are low fat and low sugar and are not concerned about exchanges, just prepare the recipes. Don't worry about the exchange information on the bottom of each recipe.

However, if you are curious about the exchange system way of eating, the following will give you a brief overview of the concept.

The idea is to divide foods into basic food groups. The foods found in each group are comparable in nutritional and caloric values. The food groups include Proteins, Breads, Vegetables, Fats, Fruits, Milk, Free Foods and Optional Calories.

If you want to lose weight, you should consult your physician or other weight control expert regarding the number of servings that would be best for YOU from each food group. Since men require more exchanges than women and children's requirements are different from adults, you can see the desired number of exchanges for any one person is a personal decision.

And as always, if you are a diabetic or have heart problems, it is best to visit with your physician before using this or any other food program or recipe collection.

PROTEINS

The foods in the Protein group include meat, poultry, seafood, eggs, cheese and legumes.

Examples of 1 protein exchange:

  1 oz of cooked weight meat, poultry or seafood

  1 egg

  3/4 oz cheese

  1/3 cup low fat cottage cheese
      or 1/2 cup fat free cottage cheese

  2 oz cooked or 3/4 oz uncooked dry beans

1 exchange of Protein is approximately 70 calories

BREADS

The foods in the Bread group include breads, crackers, cereals, grains and starchy vegetables.

Examples of 1 bread exchange:

  1 slice bread or 2 slices reduced calorie bread
      (40 calories or less)

  1/2 cup cooked pasta or rice

  3 Tablespoons flour

  3/4 oz cereal

  1/2 cup corn or peas

1 exchange of Bread is approximately 80 calories

FRUITS

The foods in the Fruit group include all fruits and fruit juices.

Examples of 1 fruit exchange:

- 1 small apple
- 1 small orange
- 1/2 medium banana
- 3/4 cup berries, except strawberries and cranberries which is 1 cup
- 1/2 cup canned fruit, packed in juice
- 2 Tablespoons Raisins

1 exchange of Fruit is approximately 60 calories

MILK

The foods in the Milk group include milk, buttermilk and yogurt.

Examples of 1 milk exchange:

- 1 cup skim milk
- 1/2 cup evaporated skim milk
- 1 cup low fat buttermilk
- 1/2 cup low fat plain yogurt or 3/4 cup plain fat free yogurt
- 1/3 cup dry skim milk powder

1 exchange of Milk is approximately 90 calories

VEGETABLE

The foods included in the Vegetable group are all vegetables other than the starchy vegetables. This includes fresh, canned or frozen vegetables.

1/2 cup of a vegetable equals 1 exchange

1 exchange of Vegetables is approximately 30 calories

FATS

The foods in the Fat group include margarine, mayonnaise, vegetable oils, salad dressings, olives and nuts.

Examples of 1 fat exchange:

- 1 teaspoon margarine or 2 teaspoons reduced calorie margarine
- 1 teaspoon vegetable oil
- 1 teaspoon mayonnaise or 2 teaspoons reduced calorie mayonnaise
- 1 teaspoon peanut butter
- 1 oz olives
- 1/4 oz pecans

1 exchange of Fat is approximately 40 calories

FREE FOODS

Foods that don't provide nutritional value, but are used to enhance the taste are included in the Free Foods. Examples are spices, herbs, extracts, vinegar, lemon juice, mustard, Worcestershire sauce and Soy sauce. Cooking sprays and artificial sweeteners used in moderation are also included in this group. However, I included the caloric value of artificial sweeteners in the optional calories breakdown of the recipes.

OPTIONAL CALORIES

Foods that don't fit into any other group, but are used in moderation in recipes are included in optional calories. Examples are sugar free gelatin and puddings, no fat mayonnaise and dressings, reduced calorie whipped toppings, reduced calorie syrups and jams, chocolate chips, coconut and canned broth.

SLIDERS

These are 80 optional calorie increments, that do not fall into any particular category. You can choose your own food group to *slide* it into. It is wise to limit this selection to 2 or 3 times a week to insure the best possible nutrition for your body while still enjoying an occasional treat.

HEALTHY EXCHANGES AND SPECIAL DIETS

By Rose Hoenig, RD, LD

The recipes in Healthy Exchanges are designed to be low in fats and sugars. This makes them very useful for persons with diabetes, heart disease or for anyone trying to eat a healthier diet. Sugar substitutes are regularly used as well as many new sugar free and low fat foods found in the local supermarket. The fat and cholesterol content of each recipe is quite low, with most recipes providing less than ten grams of fat per serving. Sodium content varies, so if you have been advised to eat less than 3000 grams of sodium per day, consult with your physician or dietitian for specific recommendations. Healthy Exchanges are intended to be used as a part of a total healthy diet with the addition of other foods to meet individual nutrient needs.

Meal planning for diabetics is based on six food groups called exchanges, published by the American Dietetic Association and The American Diabetes Association, Inc. The six groups or lists are: starch/bread, meat/protein, vegetables, fruit, milk and fat. Foods are grouped together in a list because they are alike. Every food on a list has about the same amount of carbohydrate, protein, fat and calories. Any food on a list can be exchanged or traded for any other food on the same list. These lists can be obtained from the American Diabetic Association or American Dietetic Association.

You may occasionally see a recipe that lists "free food" as part of the portion. According to the published exchange lists, a free food contains less than 20 calories per serving. Two or three servings per day of free foods/drinks is usually allowed in a meal plan.

Recipes can be calculated according to how the various ingredients fit into the six exchange lists. To simplify meal planning, exchanges less than one half are not used. This means that extra calories from various food groups may not be exactly accounted for. Generally, this will not cause a diabetic any problems unless a larger serving than the recipe gives is eaten. This is a noticeable difference from some weight loss programs.

If you are very familiar with diabetic exchanges and nutrient values of foods you may notice that amounts of carbohydrate, protein and fat given in a recipe portion do not always match what is listed in the published exchanges. This may be due to several reasons:

(1) As new foods reach the market they have been formed to be lower in fat. Sometimes small amounts of carbohydrate are added as thickeners or to add flavor and sweetness. These additions will alter the final nutrient value of that food.

(2) In some recipes there are parts of many food groups. In the exchange system portions less than 1/2 are usually not used. To simplify meal planning and to be as accurate as possible, the carbohydrate that is found in some foods may be counted as another group that also contains carbohydrate. For example, a recipe with a combination of vegetables and fruits may not contain enough of each food to equal at least 1/2 exchange but by combining the carbohydrate value of both foods the result is one whole serving of a fruit or vegetable. This method is used to help diabetics follow a typical meal plan that is developed to fit into their normal routine, without becoming too detailed.

(3) Recipes have been calculated using the diabetic exchanges and computerized nutrient analysis. Since the exchange lists are based on averages of food groups and the computer analysis is based on individual foods the total calories, carbohydrate, fat, and protein value of a recipe portion will not always match. In making a decision on what value to give a portion, this information is taken into account as well as how the average person would plan this food into their daily diet. A good recipe will provide a reasonable portion from an exchange group that would normally be eaten at a meal. One goal of diabetic meal planning is to provide flexibility, while keeping calories and carbohydrate fairly consistent. If your meal plan does not have enough exchanges to allow for the portion given, try using half the portion listed on the recipe. It is a good idea to check with your nutrition counselor before you change your meal plan.

SOME USEFUL TIDBITS IN USING THE RECIPES:

I use canned broth in place of bouillon to lower the sodium content. The intended flavor is still present in the prepared dish.

Whenever cooked rice or pasta is an ingredient, follow the package directions, but eliminate the salt and/or margarine called for. This helps lower the sodium and fat content. It tastes just fine, trust me on this.

A word of caution in regards to cooking with sugar substitutes. Use saccharin based sweeteners when heating or baking. Aspartame works well in recipes that don't require heat but leave an aftertaste in baked products.

I'm often asked why I use an 8x8 baking dish in my recipes. It's because it's much easier for portion control. If the recipe says it makes 4 servings, just cut down the center, turn the dish and cut again. Like magic, there's your serving. Also, if this is the only dish you are preparing requiring an oven, the square dish fits into a table top toaster oven easily and energy can be conserved.

You may notice, almost always when I have you open a can of something, such as tomato sauce or evaporated skim milk, I formulate the recipe around the whole can. I do this on purpose because I know many of you are like me, not perfect housekeepers and would put the unused portion away with good intentions to use it up within a day or two. But, if and when you get around to cleaning out the refrigerator, it's still sitting there.

Rarely, if ever, do I have salt as an added ingredient. So, I don't tell you to use sodium free products such as tomato sauce. But, if you have a true sodium sensitive condition, I'm trusting you to have "enough smarts" of your own to use the sodium free products, and realize recipes using high sodium ingredients, such as sauerkraut, are to be an occasional treat. I use spices and other flavor enhancing ingredients in such a way, you won't even notice the absence of salt.

To make life even easier, whenever a recipe calls for ounce measurements (other than meats) I've included the closest cup equivalent. I need to use my scale daily when creating recipes, so why not measure for you at the same time.

Unless the recipe calls for hard cooked eggs, mayonnaise, or a raw vegetable, the leftovers will freeze well. This includes most of the cream pies. Try this on individual servings for your own "TV" dinners.

Whenever I include cooked chicken in a recipe, I use roasted white meat without skin. Whenever, I include roast beef or pork in a recipe, I use the loin cuts because they are much leaner. However, most of the time, I do my roasting of all these meats at the local Deli. I just ask for a chunk of their lean roasted meat, such as 6 oz. or 8 oz. and tell them not to slice it. When I get home, I then cube or dice the meat and am ready to use in my recipe. The reason I do this is three fold. (1) I'm getting just the amount I need without leftovers (2) I don't have the expense of heating the oven (3) I'm not throwing away the bone, gristle and fat I'd be cutting away from the meat. Over all, the expense is probably cheaper to "roast" it the way I do.

After preparing many of my pies and puddings, you may notice I use nonfat dry milk powder and water in lots of the recipes. Usually I call for 2/3 cups nonfat dry milk powder and 1 1/4 to 1 1/2 cup water or liquid. I do this on purpose. I can get the nutrients of two cups of milk, but much less liquid. So, the end result is much creamier. Also, the recipe sets up quicker, usually in 5 minutes or less. So if someone is unexpectedly knocking at your door at mealtime, you can quickly throw a pie together and enjoy it minutes later.

Another trick I often use is to include tiny amounts of "real people" food, such as coconut, but extend the flavor by using extracts. Try it, you will be surprised by how little of the real thing you have to use and still feel you are not being deprived.

I am **not** a Nutritionist, Home Economist or Traditional Food Professional. But, I am probably like most of you, a 'common Jo" who enjoys normal everyday food. What I tried to do with this collection of recipes is bring back the flavor of everyday foods, but prepared in quick yet tasty low fat, low sugar and reasonably low sodium ways.

ENJOY! Lean Bon Appetite.

A PEEK INTO MY PANTRY AND MY FAVORITE BRANDS

I've been asked many times "What types of foods do you keep on hand and what brands do you use?" There are lots of good products on the grocery shelves today. Many more than we even dreamed about one year ago. And, I can't wait to see what's out there in twelve months. So, the following are my staples and where appropriate, my favorites at this time. I feel these products deliver the most flavor for the least amount of fat, sugar or calories. You may find others you like as well or better. This is only a guide to make your grocery shopping and cooking easier.

Fat Free Plain Yogurt (Yoplait)
Nonfat Dry Skim Milk Powder (Carnation)
Evaporated Skim Milk (Carnation)
Skim Milk
Fat Free Cream Cheese (Philadelphia)
Fat Free Mayonnaise (Kraft - 8 calories per tablespoon)
Fat Free Salad Dressings (Kraft)
Fat Free Sour Cream (Land O Lakes)
Reduced Calorie Margarine
    (Weight Watchers, Smart Beat or Promise)
Cooking Spray
    (Butter - Weight Watchers)(Olive and Regular - Pam)
Cooking Oil (Puritan Canola Oil)
Sugar Substitute (White - Sprinkle Sweet)
    (Brown - Sugar Twin)
Reduced Calorie Whipped Topping (Cool Whip Lite)
Sugar Free Gelatin and Pudding Mixes (Jello)
Baking Mix (Bisquick Reduced Fat)
Reduced Fat Cheese
    (Kraft, Healthy Choice and Weight Watchers)
Tomato Sauce (Hunts - regular and with tomato bits)
Shredded Frozen Potatoes (Mr. Dell's)
Spreadable Fruit (Smucker's, Welch's or Sorrell Ridge)
Peanut Butter (Jif)
Chicken Broth (Campbell's Healthy Request)
Beef Broth (Swanson)
Bacon Bits (Hormel)

Cream of Mushroom Soup (Campbell's Healthy Request)
Purchased Pie Crust (unbaked - Pillsbury - in dairy case)
     (Graham, butter flavored or chocolate - Keebler)
90% or more lean Pastrami or Corned Beef (Carl Buddig)
97% Lean Reduced Sodium Ham (Dubuque)
Lean Frankfurters & Polish Kielbasa Sausage
     (Healthy Choice)
Canned White Chicken, packed in water (Swanson)
90% Lean Ground Turkey OR Beef
Canned Tuna, packed in water
Unsweetened Apple Juice
Unsweetened Apple Sauce
Reduced Calorie Bread - 40 calories per slice or less
Hamburger Buns (Colonial Old Fashion - 80 calories per bun)
Rice - instant, regular and brown
Noodles, Spaghetti and Macaroni
Frozen Fruit - no sugar added
Fresh Fruit
Salsa
Fresh, Frozen and Canned Vegetables
Spices
Lemon and Lime Juice
Instant Lemonade (Crystal Light)

If your grocer does not stock these items, why not ask if they can try them on a trial basis. Then if the store responds, be sure to tell your friends so the sales are enough to warrant the shelf space.

The items on my shopping list are normal everyday foods, but are all as low fat and low sugar, (*while still tasting good*), as I can find. I can make any recipe in this cookbook as long as these staples are on my shelves. After using the products for a couple of weeks, you will find it becomes routine to have them on hand. And, I guarantee I DON'T spend any more now at the store than I did two years ago when I told myself I couldn't afford some of these items. But, back then, the unhealthy high priced snacks I really DIDN'T need, somehow made the magic leap from the grocery shelves into my cart. Who was I kidding?

SOUPS

SOUPS

BROCCOLI CHEESE SOUP

1/2 cup chopped onion
3 Tablespoons flour
1 1/2 cups evaporated skim milk
2 cups Campbell's Healthy Request canned chicken broth
1 (10 oz) pkg frozen chopped broccoli, thawed and
    well drained
1/2 teaspoon Worcestershire sauce
6 oz shredded reduced fat Cheddar cheese (1 1/2 cups)

In large saucepan sprayed with butter flavored cooking spray, saute onions until tender. In covered jar combine flour and evaporated skim milk. Add chicken broth, broccoli and Worcestershire sauce to onions. Gradually add milk and flour mixture. Stir constantly until thickened and broccoli is tender, about 10 minutes. Add cheese. Cook and stir until cheese melts and soup is hot. DO NOT boil.

Serves 4 (1 1/2 cups)
Each serving equals:
HE: 2 Pr, 1 3/4 Ve, 3/4 SM, 1/4 Br, 8 OC
252 calories, 8 gr Fa, 25 gr Pr, 21 gr Ca, 699 mg So
Diabetic: 2 Ve, 1 1/2 Mt, 1 SM

*This soup didn't pass **Cliff's** taste test. But, he's a member with George Bush in the "I Hate Broccoli Club". If you like broccoli, I think you'll love this soup.*

CABBAGE-RICE SOUP

4 cups Campbell's Healthy Request canned chicken broth
1/2 cup diced onion
2 cups shredded cabbage
1/2 teaspoon minced garlic
1/8 teaspoon lemon pepper
2 oz uncooked instant rice (2/3 cup)
3 oz shredded reduced fat Cheddar cheese (3/4 cup)

In large saucepan combine chicken broth, onion and shredded cabbage. Add minced garlic and lemon pepper. Simmer for 15 minutes. Add instant rice; bring to a boil, cover and remove from heat. Let set 5 minutes or until rice is done. When serving, top each bowl with 3 Tablespoons shredded cheese.

Serves 4 (1 1/2 cups)
Each serving equals:
HE: 1 1/4 Ve, 1 Pr, 1/2 Br, 16 OC
147 calories, 4 gr Fa, 12 gr Pr, 17 gr Ca, 642 mg So
Diabetic: 1 Mt, 1 St

This may be a "Plain Jane" soup to look at, but it's oh so good to eat!

LEEK AND POTATO SOUP

2 cups Campbell's Healthy Request canned chicken broth
15 oz diced raw potatoes (3 cups)
1 cup chopped onion
3 leeks, chopped
1 Tablespoon chopped parsley
1 1/2 cups evaporated skim milk
2 teaspoons reduced calorie margarine

In large saucepan bring broth to simmering. Add potatoes, onions and leeks. Cover and simmer for 20 minutes. Partially mash potatoes into broth. Add parsley, evaporated skim milk and margarine. Simmer uncovered for 3 minutes.

Serves 4 (1 1/2 cups)
Each serving equals:
HE: 3/4 Br, 3/4 SM, 1/2 Ve, 1/4 Fa, 8 OC
189 calories, 1 gr Fa, 12 gr Pr, 33 gr Ca, 363 mg So
Diabetic: 1 St, 1 Ve, 1 SM

A traditional Irish soup prepared in a non-traditional way.

TOMATO AND ASPARAGUS SOUP

1 1/2 cups chopped asparagus
4 cups Campbell's Healthy Request canned chicken broth
1/2 cup diced onion
1 teaspoon dried parsley
2 cups canned tomatoes with juice
3 Tablespoons flour
1 Tablespoon + 1 teaspoon reduced calorie margarine

In large saucepan combine asparagus, chicken broth, onion, parsley and tomatoes. Cover and simmer about 30 minutes. Place in blender and blend until smooth. Add flour and blend a few seconds more. Pour back into saucepan. Add margarine and cook slowly for another 10 minutes.

Serves 4 (1 1/2 cups)
Each serving equals:
HE: 2 Ve, 1/2 Fa, 1/4 Br, 16 OC
115 calories, 3 gr Fa, 7 gr Pr, 15 gr Ca, 1037 mg So
Diabetic: 1 St, 1/2 Fa

A pleasant blend of flavors.

SOUTHWESTERN VEGETABLE SOUP

2 cups canned tomatoes with juice
2 cups Campbell's Healthy Request canned chicken broth
1 cup shredded cabbage
1/2 cup chopped onion
1 cup frozen green beans
1 cup frozen carrots
2 teaspoons chili seasoning mix

Place tomatoes in blender; blend on puree for 10 seconds. In large saucepan combine tomatoes, chicken broth, shredded cabbage, onion, beans and carrots. Add chili seasoning. Bring to a boil. Lower heat and simmer for 45-60 minutes.

Serves 4 (1 1/2 cups)
Each serving equals:
HE: 2 3/4 Ve, 8 OC
72 calories, less than 1 gr Fa, 4 gr Pr, 13 gr Ca, 458 mg So
Diabetic: 1 St

A hint of Old Mexico in an updated soup.

GREAT NORTHERN BEAN SOUP

3 cups water
10 oz canned Great Northern Beans, rinsed and drained
5 oz diced ham (90% lean)
1 cup diced carrots
1 cup diced celery
1/2 cup diced onion
2 cups canned tomatoes with juice, coarsely chopped
1/2 cup canned sliced mushrooms, drained
1/8 teaspoon pepper
1 teaspoon dried parsley

In large saucepan combine water, beans, ham, carrots, celery, onion, tomatoes and mushrooms. Add pepper and parsley. Bring to a boil. Lower heat and simmer for about 1 hour.

HINT: 1) A 16 oz can of beans is 10 oz drained weight.

2) Dubuque 97% fat free ham works great.

Serves 4 (1 1/2 cups)
Each serving equals:
HE: 2 1/2 Pr, 2 1/2 Ve
181 calories, 2 gr Fa, 14 gr Pr, 28 gr Ca, 654 mg So
Diabetic: 2 Mt, 1 St, 1 Ve

When the winter winds blow, a pot of soup simmering on the stove is comforting to anyone coming in from the cold. Here's a filling soup to ward off the chills.

MANHATTAN BEAN SOUP

10 oz canned Great Northern beans, rinsed and drained
1 cup chopped onion
1 cup shredded carrot
3/4 cup finely chopped celery
1/8 teaspoon pepper
2 cups water
1 3/4 cups stewed tomatoes with juice, coarsely chopped
2 oz diced ham (90% lean)
1 1/2 cups evaporated skim milk

In 8 cup glass measuring bowl or large glass bowl combine beans, onion, carrot, celery, pepper and water. Cover. Microwave on 70% power (medium high) for 15 minutes. Add stewed tomatoes and diced ham. Cover and microwave additional 10 minutes on 70% power. Remove from microwave. Blend in evaporated skim milk.

HINT: 1) A 16 oz can of beans is 10 oz drained weight.

2) Dubuque 97% fat free ham works great.

Serves 4 (2 cups)
Each serving equals:
HE: 2 1/4 Ve, 1 3/4 Pr, 3/4 SM
233 calories, 1 gr Fa, 17 gr Pr, 40 gr Ca, 545 mg So
Diabetic: 1 1/2 Ve, 1 Mt, 1 SM, 1 St

This is one that gets even better the next day!

CHICKEN-CORN CHOWDER

2 cups Campbell's Healthy Request canned chicken broth
5 oz diced raw potatoes (1 cup)
1 cup diced carrots
2 cups cream style corn
8 oz diced cooked chicken breast
1 1/2 cups evaporated skim milk
1/8 teaspoon pepper
3/4 oz instant potato flakes (1/3 cup)
1 teaspoon dried parsley flakes

In large saucepan combine chicken broth, potatoes and carrots. Cover and cook over medium heat until vegetables are tender. Add cream style corn, chicken, evaporated skim milk and pepper. Stir in instant potato flakes and parsley flakes. Simmer 5 minutes.

Serves 4 (1 1/2 cups)
Each serving equals:
HE: 2 Pr, 1 1/2 Br, 3/4 SM, 1/2 Ve, 8 OC
325 calories, 3 gr Fa, 30 gr Pr, 47 gr Ca, 773 mg So
Diabetic: 2 Mt, 2 St, 1 SM, 1/2 Ve

Farmhouse taste no matter where you live!

CHINESE CHICKEN SOUP

4 cups Campbell's Healthy Request canned chicken broth
1 cup sliced celery
1/2 cup chopped onion
1/4 teaspoon minced garlic
4 oz diced cooked chicken breast
1/2 cup sliced canned mushrooms, drained
1 Tablespoon reduced sodium soy sauce
2 oz uncooked instant rice (2/3 cup)
1 (6 oz) pkg frozen snow peas
4 oz sliced water chestnuts (3/4 cup)

In large saucepan combine chicken broth, celery, onion and minced garlic. Simmer over medium heat about 10 minutes. Add chicken, mushrooms and soy sauce. Bring to a boil. Add rice, frozen snow peas and water chestnuts. Cover and remove from heat. Let set 5 minutes.

Serves 4 (1 1/2 cups)
Each serving equals:
HE: 1 1/4 Ve, 1 Pr, 3/4 Br, 16 OC
164 calories, 1 gr Fa, 15 gr Pr, 22 gr Ca, 651 mg So
Diabetic: 1 St, 1 Ve, 1 Mt

*When my friend and printer **Judy** made this soup, she said it smelled as good as it tasted. She put it all in the crockpot before she left for work and came home to the wonderful aroma.*

MIDWEST CHOWDER

5 oz diced cooked chicken breast
4 cups Campbell's Healthy Request canned chicken broth
10 oz diced raw potatoes (2 cups)
1 cup diced carrots
1 cup chopped celery
1/2 cup chopped onion
1 cup cream style corn
1 1/2 cups evaporated skim milk
3 Tablespoons flour
3 oz shredded reduced fat Cheddar cheese (3/4 cup)
1/4 teaspoon pepper
1 teaspoon dried parsley

In large saucepan combine chicken, chicken broth, potatoes, carrots, celery and onion. Cook over medium heat until vegetables are tender, about 20-25 minutes. Stir in cream style corn. In covered jar combine evaporated skim milk and flour. Stir into chicken mixture. Add cheese, pepper and parsley. Cook, stirring constantly, until cheese melts.

Serves 4 (1 1/2 cups)
Each serving equals:
HE: 2 1/4 Pr, 1 1/4 Br, 1 1/4 Ve, 3/4 SM, 18 OC
353 calories, 6 gr Fa, 32 gr Pr, 45 gr Ca, 995 mg So
Diabetic: 2 St, 2 Mt, 1 SM

*My sister-in-law, **Loretta** really liked this down home chowder. Maybe you and your family would also.*

SOUTHWESTERN CHICKEN TOMATO SOUP

2 cups Campbell's Healthy Request canned chicken broth
4 oz diced cooked chicken breast
2 cups canned tomatoes with juice, chopped
1/2 cup salsa
1 teaspoon Taco seasoning mix
1/2 cup diced onion
1 oz corn chips, coarsely chopped (scant 1/2 cup)
3/4 oz shredded reduced fat Cheddar Cheese
   (3 Tablespoons)

In large saucepan combine chicken broth, chicken, tomatoes with juice, salsa, Taco seasoning and diced onion. Simmer for about 30 minutes. Add corn chips and cook about 5 minutes longer. Ladle into 4 soup bowls and top evenly with shredded cheese just before serving.

Serves 4 (1 1/4 cups)
Each serving equals:
HE: 1 1/2 Ve, 1 1/4 Pr, 1/4 Br, 1/2 Sl
145 calories, 4 gr Fa, 14 gr Pr, 13 gr Ca, 654 mg So
Diabetic: 3 Ve, 1 Mt

Cliff *loved the flavor of this soup.*

CHILI

12 oz ground turkey or beef (90% lean)
1 cup chopped onion
1 cup chopped celery
1 cup chopped green pepper
4 cups canned tomatoes with juice, chopped
1/4 teaspoon minced garlic
2 teaspoons chili seasoning mix
10 oz canned chili beans, drained weight
1 3/4 cups canned beef broth

In large saucepan sprayed with cooking spray, saute ground meat, onion, celery and green pepper until meat is browned and vegetables tender. Add tomatoes, garlic, chili seasoning mix, chili beans with juice and beef broth. Simmer for about 1 hour.

HINT: 16 oz can of chili beans is 10 oz drained weight

Serves 6 (1 1/2 cups)

Each serving equals:
HE: 2 1/3 Pr, 2 1/3 Ve, 6 OC
208 calories, 6 gr Fa, 16 gr Pr, 23 gr Ca, 592 mg So
Diabetic: 2 Mt, 1 Ve, 1 St

*When **Phyllis** asked me to find a chili recipe for her, I created this. She called back to say it was "very good" and for sure it didn't taste diet.*

ITALIAN NOODLE SOUP

8 oz ground turkey or beef (90% lean)
1/4 cup chopped onion
1 3/4 cups canned beef broth
1 3/4 cups Italian stewed tomatoes with juice
3 oz uncooked noodles (scant 2 cups)
1/8 teaspoon pepper
3/4 oz shredded Parmesan cheese (1/4 cup)

In large saucepan sprayed with olive flavored cooking spray, brown meat and onions. Add beef broth, stewed tomatoes, noodles and pepper. Lower heat and simmer 20-30 minutes. Sprinkle each bowl with 1 Tablespoon Parmesan cheese just before serving.

Serves 4 (1 1/2 cups)
Each serving equals:
HE: 1 3/4 Pr, 1 Ve, 1 Br, 9 OC
257 calories, 8 gr Fa, 18 gr Pr, 28 gr Ca, 816 mg So
Diabetic: 2 Mt, 1 St, 1 Ve

A quick way to go on vacation without leaving home!

ITALIAN VEGETABLE SOUP

8 oz ground turkey or beef (90% lean)
3/4 cup chopped onion
1/8 teaspoon pepper
1/2 teaspoon oregano
1 3/4 cups Italian stewed tomatoes with juice, chopped
1 3/4 cups canned beef broth
1 cup frozen green beans
1 cup frozen sliced carrots
1 1/2 oz uncooked medium noodles (scant 1 cup)

In large saucepan sprayed with olive flavored cooking spray, brown meat and onion. Add pepper and oregano. Stir in tomatoes, broth, green beans and carrots. Bring to a boil. Reduce heat. Add noodles. Cover and simmer 15 minutes or until noodles and vegetables are tender.

Serves 4 (1 1/2 cups)
Each serving equals:
HE: 2 1/4 Ve, 1 1/2 Pr, 1/2 Br, 9 OC
207 calories, 6 gr Fa, 15 gr Pr, 24 gr Ca, 726 mg So
Diabetic: 2 Ve, 1 1/2 Mt, 1 St

Who says veggies don't taste good? Try this soup, it will make a vegetable lover out of anyone.

PEANUT PORK SOUP

1 1/2 cups V-8 vegetable juice
1 3/4 cups canned beef broth
4 cups purchased stir fry vegetables
6 oz cooked lean pork roast, diced
1/4 teaspoon pepper
2 Tablespoons reduced sodium soy sauce
2 oz uncooked instant rice (2/3 cup)
2 Tablespoons chunky peanut butter

In large saucepan combine vegetable juice and beef broth. Bring to a boil. Add vegetables, diced pork and pepper. Cook just until vegetables are crisp-tender, about 5 minutes. Remove from heat. Add soy sauce, instant rice and peanut butter. Stir well to blend. Cover and let set 5 minutes before serving.

Serves 4 (1 1/2 cups)
Each serving equals:
HE: 2 3/4 Ve, 2 Pr, 1/2 Br, 1/2 Fa, 9 OC
307 calories, 11 gr Fa, 20 gr Pr, 32 gr Ca, 1800 mg So
Diabetic: 3 Ve, 2 Mt, 2 St

Don't discount the peanut butter in this soup before you try it...

SEAFOOD PASTA CHOWDER

3/4 cup fresh mushrooms, sliced
3 cups skim milk
1 (1 oz) packet Newburg Sauce Mix
1/4 cup green onions, sliced 1/8"
2 cups cooked shell macaroni
5 oz crabmeat or shrimp, frozen or canned
   (rinsed and drained)
2 Tablespoons chopped fresh parsley

Spray large saucepan with butter flavored cooking spray. Saute mushrooms for 3 minutes, stirring constantly. Add milk and sauce mix. Stir well with a wire whisk over moderate heat until mixture comes to a boil. Reduce heat and simmer 5-8 minutes, stirring constantly. Add green onions, cooked macaroni and crabmeat or shrimp. Stir to combine. Sprinkle with parsley. Serve immediately.

HINT: If you can't find Newburg Sauce Mix, use Tuna Sauce Mix and 1/2 teaspoon Sherry extract.

Serves 4 (1 1/2 cups)
Each serving equals:
HE: 1 Br, 3/4 SM, 2/3 Pr, 1/2 Ve, 25 OC
269 calories, 5 gr Fa, 19 gr Pr, 37 gr Ca, 601 mg So
Diabetic: 1 Mt, 1 St, 1 SM

A wonderful way to enjoy seafood.

SALADS

SALADS

BING CHERRY-COKE SALAD

1 cup crushed pineapple, packed in its own juice, undrained
1 (4 serving) pkg sugar free cherry gelatin
1 (4 serving) pkg sugar free lemon gelatin
1 (12 oz) can Diet Coke
12 oz bing cherries, pitted and sliced (2 cups)

In medium saucepan heat pineapple with juice to boiling. Remove from heat. Stir in dry cherry and lemon gelatins, mixing well. Add Diet Coke and sliced bing cherries. Mix to combine. Pour into an 8x8 dish. Chill until set.

Serves 6
Each serving equals:
HE: 1 Fr, 11 OC
74 Calories, less than 1 gr Fa, 3 gr Pr, 16 gr Ca, 8 mg So
Diabetic: 1 Fr

A pleasant way to enjoy the flavor of Bing cherries.

CHERRY WALDORF SALAD

1 (4 serving) pkg sugar free cherry gelatin
1 cup boiling water
1/2 cup cold water
1 small apple, cored and diced (1/2 cup)
1 medium banana, diced
3/4 cup chopped celery
1 1/2 oz chopped walnuts (1/3 cup)

In medium bowl dissolve gelatin in boiling water. Add cold water. Chill until partially set. Add apple, banana, celery and walnuts. Stir gently to blend. Pour into 8x8 dish. Chill until set. When serving, good topped with 1 Tablespoon reduced calorie whipped topping. If using, count optional calories accordingly.

Serves 6
Each serving equals:
HE: 1/2 Fr, 1/2 Fa, 1/4 Ve, 1/4 Pr, 5 OC
85 calories, 4 gr Fa, 2 gr Pr, 10 gr Ca, 50 mg So
Diabetic: 1/2 Fr, 1 Fa

And you thought Waldorf salad only meant apples.

CRANBERRY APPLE RELISH

3 cups fresh cranberries
3 small apples, cored and finely chopped (1 1/2 cup)
3/4 cup finely chopped celery
1 1/2 oz chopped walnuts (1/3 cup)
1 (4 serving) pkg sugar free lemon gelatin
4 Tablespoons Sprinkle Sweet

In food processor or grinder, coarsely chop cranberries. In large bowl combine cranberry and apples. Blend in celery and walnuts. Add dry lemon gelatin and Sprinkle Sweet. Mix well to combine. Cover and chill at least 6-8 hours before using.

Serves 6 (2/3 cup)
Each serving equals:
HE: 1 Fr, 1/2 Fa, 1/4 Pr, 1/4 Ve, 9 OC
131 calories, 5 gr Fa, 2 gr Pr, 20 gr Ca, 52 mg So
Diabetic: 1 Fr, 1 Fa

This is so easy and tasty don't save it only for Thanksgiving.

FESTIVE RASPBERRY CROWN SALAD

1 (8 oz) pkg fat free cream cheese
1 1/2 cups evaporated skim milk
1/2 teaspoon almond extract
Sugar substitute to equal 2 Tablespoons sugar
1 3/4 cups boiling water
1 (4 serving) pkg sugar free lemon gelatin
1 (4 serving) pkg sugar free raspberry gelatin
3 cups fresh raspberries
   or frozen, thawed and well drained

In medium bowl stir cream cheese with spoon until fluffy. Add 1 cup evaporated skim milk, almond extract and sugar substitute. Mix well. In small bowl combine 1 cup boiling water and dry lemon gelatin. Add to cream cheese mixture, blending well. Pour into 8x8 dish. Chill until set. In medium bowl combine remaining 3/4 cup boiling water and dry raspberry gelatin. Blend in remaining 1/2 cup evaporated skim milk and raspberries. Chill until partially set. Stir occasionally to prevent fruit from floating to the top. Pour over set cream cheese layer. Continue chilling until set. When serving, good topped with 1 Tablespoon reduced calorie whipped topping. If using, count optional calories accordingly.

HINT: 3 cups frozen raspberries, thawed and drained, can
      be substituted for fresh

Serves 6
Each serving equals:
HE: 2/3 Pr, 2/3 Fr, 1/2 SM, 13 OC
124 calories, less than 1 gr Fa, 13 gr Pr, 17 gr Ca, 373 mg So
Diabetic: 1/2 Mt, 1/2 Fr, 1/2 SM

This is so pretty you may hesitate to cut into it. But, please do. You'll be glad you did.

FRESH STRAWBERRY-BANANA SALAD

1 (4 serving) pkg sugar free instant vanilla pudding mix
1 cup water
1/2 cup reduced calorie whipped topping
   (8 calories per Tablespoon)
1/4 teaspoon coconut extract
2 cups fresh strawberries, sliced
1 medium banana, diced

In medium bowl combine pudding mix, water, whipped topping and coconut extract. Mix well using a wire whisk. Add sliced strawberries and diced banana. Mix gently to combine. Cover and chill until ready to serve.

Serves 4 (1/2 cup)
Each serving equals:
HE: 1 Fr, 1/2 Sl, 1 OC
89 calories, 1 gr Fa, 1 gr Pr, 20 gr Ca, 321 mg So
Diabetic: 1 Fr

My all time favorite food is strawberries. This salad does the fruit proud.

RHUBARB-STRAWBERRY JELLO SALAD

4 cups diced fresh or frozen rhubarb
1/2 cup water
1/4 cup Sprinkle Sweet
2 (4 serving) pkgs sugar free strawberry gelatin
1/2 cup cold water
1 cup fresh or frozen strawberries, no sugar added

In a saucepan combine rhubarb, 1/2 cup water and Sprinkle Sweet. Cook over medium heat until rhubarb is tender. Pour rhubarb into large bowl and stir in dry gelatin. Stir until dissolved. Add 1/2 cup cold water. Cool slightly and fold in strawberries. Pour into 8 x 8 dish. Chill until set.

Serves 4
Each serving equals:
HE: 2 Ve, 1/4 Fr, 22 OC
60 calories, less than 1 gr Fa, 4 gr Pr, 11 gr Ca, 117 mg So
Diabetic: 1 Fr

Diane sent in a refreshing way to enjoy the first "fruits" of spring.

PEANUT BUTTER WALDORF SALAD

2 small red apples, cored and chopped (1 cup)
1/4 cup raisins
1 cup chopped celery
3/4 cup plain fat free yogurt
3 Tablespoons chunky peanut butter
2 teaspoons vanilla extract
Sugar substitute to equal 3 Tablespoons sugar

In medium bowl combine apples, raisins and celery. In small bowl combine yogurt, peanut butter, vanilla and sugar substitute. Mix well. Pour over apple mixture. Toss gently to combine. Cover and chill.

Serves 4 (3/4 cup)
Each serving equals:
HE: 1 Fr, 1/2 Ve, 3/4 Pr, 3/4 Fa, 1/4 SM, 2 OC
178 calories, 6 gr Fa, 6 gr Pr, 27 gr Ca, 135 mg So
Diabetic: 2 Fr, 1 Mt, 1/2 Fa

If you like peanut butter, you will love this salad.

TAFFY APPLE SALAD

1 (4 serving) pkg sugar free cook and serve vanilla
   pudding mix
1 (4 serving) pkg sugar free Hawaiian- Pineapple gelatin
1 cup water
1 Tablespoon white or apple cider vinegar
4 small apples, cored and chopped (2 cups)
1 cup crushed pineapple, packed in its own juice, drained
1 oz chopped pecans (1/4 cup)
1 1/2 cups reduced calorie whipped topping
   (8 calories per Tablespoon)

In small saucepan combine pudding mix, dry gelatin, water
and vinegar. Bring to a boil, stirring constantly. Remove
from heat and refrigerate until cool. Combine chopped
apples, pineapple and walnuts. Stir in cooled pudding
mixture. Gently fold in whipped topping. Chill until ready to
serve.

Serves 8 (2/3 cup)
Each serving equals:
HE: 3/4 Fr, 1/2 Fa, 38 OC
111 calories, 4 gr Fa, 1 gr Pr, 19 gr Ca, 97 mg So
Diabetic: 1 Fr, 1 Fa

*If you like taffy apples on a stick, this is just as good, and
better for you.*

PEAR LIME SALAD

8 pear halves, packed in fruit juice, drained
(reserve 1 cup juice)
1 (4 serving) pkg sugar free lime gelatin
1 cup cold water
1 (8 oz) pkg fat free cream cheese, softened to
room temperature
1 cup reduced calorie whipped topping
(8 calories per Tablespoon)

Heat 1 cup pear juice. Add dry gelatin and 1 cup cold
water. Blend well. Chill until thickened. Put pears in
blender and chop for 5-6 seconds. Add cream cheese.
Blend until smooth. Add gelatin mixture and whipped
topping. Blend a few seconds. Pour into 8x8 dish. Chill
until set.

Serves 4
Each serving equals:
HE: 1 Pr, 1 Fr, 1/2 Sl
153 calories, 2 gr Fa, 10 gr Pr, 23 gr Ca, 399 mg So
Diabetic: 1 Mt, 1 1/2 Fr

*My friend **Faye** shared this recipe. She said if you pour the
salad into a prepared pie shell it tastes just like Key Lime
Pie!*

QUICK CARROT RAISIN SALAD

1/4 cup raisins
2 cups grated carrots
1 cup pineapple tidbits, packed in its own juice, drained
1/4 cup no fat mayonnaise (8 calories per Tablespoon)
2 teaspoons lemon juice

In medium bowl combine raisins, carrots and pineapple.
Blend in mayonnaise and lemon juice. Gently combine.
Serve on salad greens.

Serves 4 (1/2 cup)
Each serving equals:
HE: 1 Fr, 1 Ve, 8 OC
101 Calories, 0 gr Fa, 1 gr Pr, 27 gr Ca, 147 mg So
Diabetic: 1 Fr, 1 Ve

Not only does it taste good, it goes together in seconds.

CARROT AND APPLE SALAD

4 oz fat free cream cheese, softened
3 Tablespoons fat free mayonnaise
   (8 calories per Tablespoon)
2 teaspoons lemon juice
2 small apples, cored and chopped (1 cup)
2 cups shredded carrots
1/4 cup raisins
1/8 teaspoon nutmeg

In medium bowl stir cream cheese with spoon until fluffy. Stir in mayonnaise and lemon juice. Add apples, carrots and raisins. Mix well to coat. Sprinkle lightly with nutmeg. Cover and chill until ready to serve.

Serves 4 (3/4 cup)
Each serving equals:
HE: 1 Fr, 1 Ve, 1/2 Pr, 6 OC
127 calories, 0 gr Fa, 5 gr Pr, 27 gr Ca, 285 mg So
Diabetic: 1 Fr, 1 Ve, 1/2 Mt

An easy way to enjoy the beta carotene of veggies and dried fruit.

CUCUMBER POTATO SALAD

12 oz thinly sliced cooked potatoes (2 1/4 cups)
1/2 cup thinly sliced radishes
1/4 cup thinly sliced red onion
3/4 cup thinly sliced cucumber
1/3 cup fat free mayonnaise (8 calories per Tablespoon)
1/4 teaspoon lemon pepper
Sugar substitute to equal 4 teaspoons sugar

In large bowl combine potatoes, radishes, onion and cucumbers. Add mayonnaise, lemon pepper and sugar substitute. Mix gently. Cover and refrigerate several hours before serving.

Serves 4 (3/4 cup)
Each serving equals:
HE: 1 Br, 3/4 Ve, 13 OC
92 calories, 0 gr Fa, 2 gr Pr, 22 gr Ca, 171 mg So
Diabetic: 1 St, 1 Ve

This is a refreshing salad using cucumbers with traditional potatoes.

ITALIAN TOMATO SALAD

4 medium tomatoes, cut into chunks
1/2 cup diced onion
1/2 cup diced green pepper
2 oz sliced black olives (1/2 cup)
1/2 cup fat free Italian Dressing
   (4 calories per Tablespoon)

In large low sided bowl, combine tomatoes, onion, green pepper and olives. Pour dressing over top. Gently stir to combine. Cover and chill.

Serves 6 (3/4 cup)
Each serving equals:
HE: 1 Ve, 1/3 Fa, 5 OC
41 calories, 1 gr Fa, 1 gr Pr, 7 gr Ca, 256 mg So
Diabetic: 1 Ve

I've never met a man yet who didn't like this salad.

SUMMER CORN SALAD

2 cups frozen corn, thawed
1/4 cup chopped green pepper
1/4 cup onion
1/4 cup cucumber
1/4 cup shredded carrots
1 1/2 oz shredded reduced fat Cheddar cheese (1/3 cup)
2 Tablespoons sweet pickle relish
1/3 cup fat free Thousand Island Dressing
    (16 calories per Tablespoon)

In large bowl combine corn, green pepper, onion,
cucumber, carrots, cheese and pickle relish. Add
Thousand Island Dressing. Mix well to combine. Cover
and chill until ready to serve.

Serves 4 (3/4 cup)
Each serving equals:
HE; 1 Br, 1/2 Ve, 1/2 Pr, 29 OC
155 calories, 3 gr Fa, 6 gr Pr, 26 gr Ca, 323 mg So
Diabetic: 1 1/2 St, 1/2 Mt

*A wonderful salad to enjoy anytime of the year, but
especially in the heat of the summer.*

ZUCCHINI SALAD BOWL

1 cup sliced zucchini
8 oz cooked potatoes, peeled and diced (1 1/2 cups)
1 cup frozen peas, thawed
1 cup diced cooked carrots
1/2 cup fat free Ranch Dressing
    (20 calories per Tablespoon)
1 Tablespoon sweet pickle relish
1/8 teaspoon pepper

In medium bowl combine zucchini, potatoes, peas and carrots. Add Ranch Dressing, pickle relish and pepper. Toss gently to combine. Cover and chill until ready to serve.

Serves 8 (full 1/2 cup)
Each serving equals:
HE: 1/2 Br, 1/2 Ve, 22 OC
72 calories, 0 gr Fa, 2 gr Pr, 16 gr Ca, 199 mg So
Diabetic: 1 St

When you swear the zucchini is taking over the world, try this salad. It won't get rid of your bumper crop, but every little bit helps.

MOLDED RELISH SALAD

1 (4 serving) pkg sugar free lime gelatin
1 cup hot water
1 cup cold water
2 Tablespoons cider vinegar
1 teaspoon prepared horseradish
1/8 teaspoon pepper
1 cup chopped cabbage
1/2 cup chopped cucumber
1/2 cup shredded carrot
2 Tablespoons chopped green pepper
2 Tablespoons chopped radishes
Lettuce

In medium size bowl dissolve gelatin in hot water. Stir in cold water. Add vinegar, horseradish and pepper. Blend well. Add cabbage, cucumber, carrot, green pepper and radishes. Mix well. Pour into 8x8 dish. Chill until firm. When serving, place on lettuce lined salad plates. Good topped with 1 teaspoon no fat mayonnaise. If using, count optional calories accordingly.

Serves 8
Each serving equals:
HE: 2/3 Ve, 4 OC
12 calories, 0 gr Fa, 1 gr Pr, 2 gr Ca, 32 mg So
Diabetic: 1 Free Ve

An updated version of one of my mother's salads.

PEA AND CHEESE SALAD

3 cups frozen peas, thawed
1/2 cup sliced celery
1/4 cup chopped onion
3 oz shredded reduced fat Cheddar cheese (3/4 cup)
1 Tablespoon bacon bits
1/2 cup fat free Ranch Dressing
   (20 calories per Tablespoon)

In medium bowl combine peas, celery, onion, cheese, bacon bits and Ranch dressing. Mix well. Cover and chill 2 hours before serving.

Serves 6 (3/4 cup)
Each serving equals:
HE: 1 Br, 2/3 Pr, 1/4 Ve, 32 OC
128 calories, 3 gr Fa, 9 gr Pr, 17 gr Ca, 422 mg So
Diabetic: 1 St, 1/2 Mt

*My sister **Mary** said this is as good or better as any she has eaten in a restaurant.*

GAZPACHO SALAD

1 3/4 cups Italian stewed tomatoes with juice
1 cup diced cucumber
3/4 cup sliced celery
1 teaspoon vegetable oil
1/4 teaspoon minced garlic
2 cups cooked Garden Style Twirl noodles

In large bowl combine stewed tomatoes, cucumber, celery, vegetable oil and minced garlic. Add cooked noodles. Mix gently. Cover and chill.

Serves 4 (1 cup)
Each serving equals:
HE: 1 3/4 Ve, 1 Br, 1/4 Fa
144 calories, 2 gr Fa, 5 gr Pr, 28 gr Ca, 298 mg So
Diabetic: 1 Ve, 1 St

When it's your turn to bring the salad to a potluck, give this one a try. You'll be glad you did.

LETTUCE BEET SALAD

4 cups shredded lettuce
1 1/2 cups julienne cut canned beets
1/2 cup finely diced onion
1/2 cup fat free Ranch Dressing
   (20 calories per Tablespoon)

On 4 salad plates, arrange 1 cup of shredded lettuce 2/3 across the plate. Evenly divide the julienne beets on the remaining 1/3 of the plate. Sprinkle 2 Tablespoons of diced onion on top of each serving. Garnish each with 2 Tablespoons Ranch dressing. Chill until ready to serve.

Serves 4
Each serving equals:
HE: 3 Ve, 1/2 Sl
70 calories, 0 gr Fa, 1 gr Pr, 16 gr Ca, 480 mg So
Diabetic: 3 Ve

Bernita *shares a recipe that hit the Jackpot with many who tried it. Is it only coincidence she first tried this salad in Las Vegas?*

CONTINENTAL RICE SALAD

2 cups cooked rice
1 cup frozen peas, thawed
3 oz shredded reduced fat Swiss cheese (3/4 cup)
1/4 cup minced pimento
1/4 cup diced celery
1/4 cup green onion, sliced
2 teaspoons bacon bits
1/3 cup fat free mayonnaise (8 calories per Tablespoon)
1 Tablespoon Dijon mustard
1/2 teaspoon lemon pepper

In medium bowl combine rice, peas, Swiss cheese, pimento, celery, onion and bacon bits. Add mayonnaise, mustard and lemon pepper. Mix gently to blend. Chill until ready to serve. Fluff with a fork just before serving.

Serves 6 (2/3 cup)
Each serving equals:
HE; 1 Br, 2/3 Pr, 1/4 Ve, 10 OC
160 calories, 4 gr Fa, 6 gr Pr, 26 gr Ca, 443 mg So
Diabetic: 1 1/2 St, 1/2 Mt

*When **Karen** requested a side dish using rice, this salad was born.*

TURKEY AND CHEDDAR PASTA SALAD

2 cups cooked elbow macaroni, rinsed and drained
2 cups cooked frozen green beans, drained
6 oz diced cooked turkey breast
3 oz shredded reduced fat Cheddar cheese (3/4 cup)
1/8 teaspoon lemon pepper
2 Tablespoons diced pimento
1/4 cup Fat Free Honey Dijon Ranch Dressing
   (20 calories per Tablespoon)
1 teaspoon dried parsley flakes

In large bowl combine macaroni, green beans, turkey, cheese, lemon pepper and pimento. Stir in dressing and parsley flakes. Toss until well mixed. Chill at least 2 hours before serving.

Serves 4 (1 1/4 cups)
Each serving equals:
HE: 2 1/2 Pr, 1 Br, 1 Ve, 20 OC
257 Calories, 6 gr Fa, 24 gr Pr, 27 gr Ca, 339 mg So
Diabetic: 2 Mt, 1 St, 1 Ve

A meal in itself.

FRANKFURTER, LETTUCE AND TOMATO SALAD

6 oz Healthy Choice frankfurters (97% lean)
4 cups finely shredded lettuce
2 medium tomatoes, diced
1/3 cup fat free Thousand Island Dressing
  (16 calories per Tablespoon)
4 slices reduced calorie Italian Bread (40 calories per slice)

Dice frankfurters and brown in skillet sprayed with cooking spray. Remove from heat and cool. In large bowl combine shredded lettuce and diced tomatoes. Add cooled frankfurters and Thousand Island Dressing. Mix gently to combine. Toast bread. Quickly spray toast with butter flavored cooking spray. Dice toast into small pieces. Add to lettuce mixture and toss gently.

Serves 4 (2 cups)
Each serving equals:
HE: 2 1/2 Ve, 1 Pr, 1/2 Br, 21 OC
128 calories, 1 gr Fa, 10 gr Pr, 21 gr Ca, 703 mg So
Diabetic: 1 1/2 Ve, 1 Mt, 1 St

*An unusual combination of foods, but worth experimenting with. At least that's what **Cliff** said.*

VEGETABLES

VEGETABLES

ASPARAGUS AND MUSHROOMS
WITH LEMON BUTTER

1/2 lb fresh asparagus spears or 1 (8 oz) pkg
   frozen cut asparagus
2 Tablespoons reduced calorie margarine
1 teaspoon sesame seeds
1 1/2 cups fresh mushrooms, sliced
2 teaspoons lemon juice

Place 2-3 tablespoons water in 8x8 baking dish. Add
asparagus spears. Cover. Microwave on high for 7-9
minutes, stirring at least once during cooking time. Let
stand 3 minutes. Meanwhile place 1 Tablespoon
margarine in custard cup. Microwave on high 30-60
seconds or until melted. Stir in sesame seeds. Micro on
high 3-4 minutes or until brown, stirring once. Set aside.
Sprinkle mushrooms over asparagus. Cover. Microwave
on high for 1 minute. Set aside. Melt remaining 1
Tablespoon margarine in small dish on high until melted.
Stir in lemon juice. Drain vegetables. Add sesame seeds
and lemon butter; mix gently to coat. Serve at once.

Serves 4
Each serving equals:
HE: 1 1/2 Ve, 3/4 Fa, 8 OC
42 calories, 2 gr Fa, 2 gr Pr, 4 gr Ca, 28 mg So
Diabetic: 1 Ve, 1/2 Fa

Micro magic at it's best.

ADOBE BEAN AND CARROT TOSS

2 cups canned sliced carrots, drained
2 cups canned green beans, drained
1 1/2 oz shredded reduced fat Cheddar cheese (1/3 cup)
1/2 cup chunky salsa
1/2 cup fat free Catalina Dressing
    (18 calories per Tablespoon)

In large bowl combine carrots, green beans and cheese. In small bowl combine salsa and Catalina dressing. Pour over vegetables. Toss to coat. Cover and refrigerate at least 2 hours.

Serves 4 (1 cup)
Each serving equals:
HE: 2 1/4 Ve, 1/2 Pr, 36 OC
108 calories, 2 gr Fa, 5 gr Pr, 18 gr Ca, 843 mg So
Diabetic: 3 Ve or 1 St

A new way with old standbys.

BREEZY GREEN BEANS

6 cups canned French style green beans, drained
1 (8 oz) pkg fat free cream cheese
1/4 teaspoon Lemon pepper

In large saucepan combine beans, cream cheese and
pepper. Heat over medium heat until cream cheese melts,
stirring often.

Serves 8 (2/3 cup)
Each serving equals:
HE: 1 1/2 Ve, 1/2 Pr
45 calories, 0 gr Fa, 5 gr Pr, 6 gr Ca, 423 mg So
Diabetic: 1 Ve, 1/2 Mt

These are a breeze to make, thus the name.

GRANDE GREEN BEANS

1/2 cup chopped onions
3 cups frozen French style green beans
1/8 teaspoon lemon pepper
1/2 cup canned sliced mushrooms, drained
1 1/2 oz shredded reduced fat Monterey Jack
    or Cheddar cheese (1/3 cup)

In medium saucepan sprayed with butter flavored cooking spray, cook onions until tender. Add beans and lemon pepper. Cover. Cook, stirring occasionally, until beans are thawed and separated, about 10 minutes. Remove cover. Add mushrooms, continue cooking, stirring occasionally until beans are just tender, about 5 minutes. Sprinkle with cheese. Cover and let stand 1 minute before serving.

Serves 4 (1 1/4 cup)
Each serving equals:
HE: 2 Ve, 1/2 Pr
65 calories, 2 gr Fa, 5 gr Pr, 7 gr Ca, 457 mg So
Diabetic: 2 Ve

A woman wrote me to say her husband said he didn't know green beans could taste this good!

GREEN BEANS WITH MUSHROOMS

2 Tablespoons minced onions
2 cups canned green beans, drained
2 Tablespoons chopped pimento
1 teaspoon minced parsley
1/2 cup canned sliced mushrooms, drained
1/8 teaspoon lemon pepper

In medium skillet sprayed with butter flavored cooking spray, saute onion until tender. Add beans, pimento, parsley, mushrooms and lemon pepper. Continue cooking until beans are heated.

Serves 2 (1 full cup)
Each serving equals:
HE: 2 3/4 Ve
48 calories, 0 gr Fa, 3 gr Pr 10 gr Ca, 581 mg So
Diabetic: 2 Ve

A touch of style with ingredients always on hand.

BROCCOLI-CORN DISH

1 (10 oz) pkg frozen broccoli, thawed
2 cups cream style corn
1/2 cup evaporated skim milk
1 egg, slightly beaten, or equivalent in egg substitute
1/2 teaspoon lemon pepper
3/4 oz corn flakes, crushed (1/2 cup)

Preheat oven to 350 degrees. Combine thawed broccoli and corn in medium bowl. In small bowl add milk to slightly beaten egg. Pour over broccoli and corn mixture. Add lemon pepper. Mix well to blend. Pour into 8x8 baking dish sprayed with butter flavored cooking spray. Sprinkle top with crushed corn flakes. Quickly spray with butter flavored spray. Bake 30 minutes.

Serves 4
Each serving equals:
HE: 1 1/2 Ve, 1 1/4 Br, 1/4 Pr (limited), 1/4 SM
189 calories, 2 gr Fa, 8 gr Pr, 35 gr Ca, 491 mg So
Diabetic: 2 St, 1 1/2 Ve

*I loved this. **Cliff** hated it. You decide.*

MICROWAVE CORN FILLED TOMATOES

4 large tomatoes
1 Tablespoon + 1 teaspoon reduced calorie margarine
1/4 cup chopped onion
1/4 cup chopped green pepper
1 1/2 cups frozen or fresh whole kernel corn
3/4 oz grated Parmesan cheese (1/4 cup)

Cut tops off tomatoes; hollow out inside. Place tomatoes in 8x8 baking dish. Combine margarine, onion, bell pepper and corn in 4 cup glass measuring cup. Microwave on medium power 4-5 minutes. Spoon corn mixture into tomatoes. Sprinkle 1 Tablespoon Parmesan cheese over each. Microwave on high 6-7 minutes or until heated through. Let stand 3 minutes before serving.

Serves 4
Each serving equals:
HE: 1 1/2 Ve, 3/4 Br, 1/2 Fa, 1/4 Pr
127 calories, 4 gr Fa, 5 gr Pr, 18 gr Ca, 136 mg So
Diabetic: 1 Ve, 1 St, 1/2 Mt

*My sister **Mary** said these quickly became a favorite.*

SWISS TOMATO-CORN BAKE

1 3/4 cups stewed tomatoes with juice
1/4 cup chopped onions
1 cup frozen whole kernel corn, thawed
1/4 teaspoon pepper
1 1/2 oz onion and sage stuffing mix (1 cup)
2 oz diced ham (90% lean)
1 1/2 oz shredded reduced fat Swiss cheese (1/3 cup)

Preheat oven to 350 degrees. In large bowl combine tomatoes, onions, corn, and pepper. Stir in stuffing mix, ham and cheese. Pour into 8x8 baking dish sprayed with butter flavored cooking spray. Bake 30 minutes.

HINT: Dubuque 97% fat free ham works great.

Serves 4
Each serving equals:
HE: 1 Br, 1 Pr, 1 Ve
163 calories, 4 gr Fa, 8 gr Pr, 24 gr Ca, 735 mg So
Diabetic: 1 St, 1 Mt, 1 Ve

Cliff enjoyed this so much, he asked me to make it again the next day.

SCALLOPED ONIONS AND CHEESE

3 cups onions, peeled, thinly sliced
   and separated into rings
3 Tablespoons water
2 Tablespoons reduced calorie margarine
2 Tablespoons flour
1 teaspoon dried parsley flakes
1/4 teaspoon dry mustard
1/8 teaspoon pepper
1 cup skim milk
1 1/2 oz shredded reduced fat Cheddar cheese (1/3 cup)

In an 8x8 micro baking dish combine onions and water. Cover and microwave on high for 5-7 minutes or until tender, stirring after 3 minutes. Set aside. Place margarine in 2 cup glass measuring cup. Microwave on high until melted, about 50 seconds. Stir in flour, parsley flakes, dry mustard and pepper. Blend in milk. Microwave on high 2-3 minutes or until thickened. Stir after 2 minutes. Drain onions and return to 8x8 baking dish. Stir in white sauce. Sprinkle cheese evenly over top. Reduce power to 50% or bake. Microwave 2-4 minutes or until cheese melts, rotating baking dish 1/2 turn after every minute.

Serves 4
Each serving equals:
HE: 1 1/2 Ve, 3/4 Fa, 1/2 Pr, 1/4 SM, 15 OC
117 calories, 4 gr Fa, 7 gr Pr, 13 gr Ca, 158 mg So
Diabetic: 2 Ve, 1/2 Fa, 1/2 Mt

For onion lovers everywhere!

GLAZED CARROTS

3 cups sliced carrots
1 Tablespoon water
1 Tablespoon + 1 teaspoon reduced calorie margarine
1 Tablespoon Orange Marmalade or Apple Jelly
   Spreadable Fruit

In 8x8 glass baking dish combine carrots and water. Cover and microwave on high 5 minutes. Let stand 6-8 minutes. Microwave on high another 4 minutes or until tender. Drain. Return carrots to dish. Dot top with margarine and spreadable fruit. Microwave on high 1-2 minutes or until margarine and spreadable fruit are melted.

Serves 4
Each serving equals:
HE: 1 1/2 Ve, 1/2 Fa, 1/4 Fr
58 calories, 1 gr Fa, 1 gr Pr, 11 gr Ca, 49 mg So
Diabetic: 2 Ve

The spreadable fruit is just the right touch to these carrots.

GARLIC TOMATO SLICES

4 medium tomatoes, cut into 1/4 inch slices
1/4 cup fat free Italian dressing
   (4 calories per Tablespoon)
2 cloves garlic, finely chopped
   or 2 teaspoons minced garlic

Place tomatoes in glass dish. In small bowl combine Italian dressing and garlic. Pour over tomatoes. Cover and refrigerate at least 3 hours. Serve on lettuce leaves, if desired.

Serves 4
Each serving equals:
HE: 1 Ve, 4 OC
32 calories, 0 gr Fa. 1 gr Pr, 7 gr Ca, 151 mg So
Diabetic: 1 Ve

Tastes great, but don't pucker up right after eating!

CALICO STOVE TOP BAKED BEANS

1 cup chopped onion
1/3 cup fat free Catalina Dressing
   (18 calories per Tablespoon)
Brown sugar substitute to equal
   3 Tablespoons brown sugar
3 Tablespoons prepared mustard
10 oz canned red kidney beans, rinsed and drained
10 oz canned butter beans, rinsed and drained
10 oz canned Great Northern beans, rinsed and drained

In large skillet sprayed with cooking spray, saute onion until tender. Stir in Catalina dressing, brown sugar substitute and mustard. Add beans. Stir well to blend. Lower heat. Cook 10 minutes or until beans are heated through, stirring occasionally.

HINT: 16 oz can of beans is 10 oz drained weight.

Serves 6 (3/4 cup)
Each serving equals:
HE: 2 1/2 Pr, 1/3 Ve, 19 OC
196 calories, 1 gr Fa, 11 gr Pr, 36 gr Ca, 348 mg So
Diabetic: 2 St, 1 1/2 Mt

This is a case of 'you just never know'. When I served this to my helpers, I never dreamed it would be the hit it was.

CANDIED SWEET POTATO BAKE

12 oz cooked sweet potatoes (2 1/4 cups)
6 oz diced ham (90% lean)
1/2 cup maple syrup (10 calories per Tablespoon)
2 eggs, slightly beaten, or equivalent in egg substitute
1/2 cup evaporated skim milk

Preheat oven to 350 degrees. In a medium bowl, mash sweet potatoes. Add diced ham. Mix well. Add maple syrup and stir to blend. In small bowl, slightly beat eggs and add milk. Pour into sweet potato mixture. Stir until well blended. Pour into 8x8 baking dish sprayed with butter flavored cooking spray. Bake 40-45 minutes or until knife inserted in center comes out clean.

HINT: Dubuque 97% fat free ham works great.

Serves 4
Each serving equals:
HE: 2 Pr (1/4 limited), 1 Br, 1/4 SM, 20 OC
144 calories, 3 gr Fa, 9 gr Pr, 20 gr Ca, 319 mg So
Diabetic: 1 Mt, 1 1/2 St

An unusual blend of flavors.

SWEET POTATO CASSEROLE

2 lbs sweet potatoes, cooked and peeled
1/2 cup evaporated skim milk
1 1/4 cups plain fat free yogurt
2 eggs or equivalent in egg substitute
Brown sugar substitute to equal 3 Tablespoons
1 1/2 teaspoons pumpkin pie spice
1/8 teaspoon pepper
2 oz walnuts (1/2 cup)

Preheat oven to 350 degrees. In medium bowl whip sweet potatoes and evaporated skim milk with electric mixer until smooth. Blend in yogurt, eggs, brown sugar substitute, pumpkin pie spice and pepper. Add walnuts, gently stirring to blend. Pour into 8x12 baking dish sprayed with butter flavored cooking spray. Bake 25-30 minutes.

Serves 8
Each serving equals:
HE: 1 Br, 1/2 Pr (1/4 limited), 1/2 Fa, 1/3 SM, 3 OC
217 calories, 6 gr Fa, 7 gr Pr, 34 gr Ca, 82 mg So
Diabetic: 2 St, 1/2 Mt, 1/2 Fa

This may be what you are looking for to go with the lean ham you are baking.

MAIN DISHES

MAIN DISHES

MACARONI AND CHEESE WITH TOMATOES

2 1/2 cups cooked elbow macaroni

1/2 cup chopped onion

1 1/2 cups evaporated skim milk

3 Tablespoons flour

4 1/2 oz shredded reduced fat Cheddar cheese
(full 1 cup)

2 Tablespoons bacon bits

2 cups canned tomatoes, drained and chopped

1/8 teaspoon pepper

1 teaspoon parsley flakes

Preheat oven to 350 degrees. In large skillet sprayed with butter flavored cooking spray, saute onions until tender. In covered jar combine evaporated skim milk and flour. Pour into skillet with onions. Add cheese and stir until sauce thickens and cheese melts. Add cooked macaroni, bacon bits, canned tomatoes, pepper and parsley flakes. Pour into 8x8 baking dish sprayed with butter flavored cooking spray. Bake 15 minutes.

Serves 4
Each serving equals:
HE: 1 1/2 Br, 1 1/2 Pr, 1 1/4 Ve, 3/4 SM, 15 OC
356 calories, 7 gr Fa, 25 gr Pr, 49 gr Ca, 622 mg So
Diabetic: 2 St, 1 1/2 Mt, 1 Ve, 1 SM

I put two of my long time favorites together and came up with a new favorite.

VEGETABLE HASH

1 2/3 cups water
1/3 cup nonfat dry milk powder
3 oz instant potato flakes (1 1/3 cups)
2 cups diced canned carrots, drained
2 cups cut canned green beans, drained
3 oz shredded reduced fat Cheddar cheese (3/4 cup)
1/8 teaspoon pepper

Preheat oven to 350 degrees. In large saucepan bring water to a boil. Remove from heat. Add dry milk powder and potato flakes. Mix lightly. Add carrots, green beans, cheese and pepper. Mix well to combine. Pour into 8x8 baking dish sprayed with butter flavored cooking spray. Lightly spray top with butter flavored cooking spray. Bake 15-20 minutes.

Serves 4
Each serving equals:
HE: 2 Ve, 1 Pr, 1 Br, 1/4 SM
191 calories, 4 gr Fa, 12 gr Pr, 27 gr Ca, 562 mg So
Diabetic: 2 Ve, 1 Mt, 1 St

*When **Tom** walked in the door hungry and I was busy, I threw this together. I only wanted something quick to feed him. I never dreamed he would say it was so good he wanted seconds!*

MEXICALI QUICHE

1 purchased 9" refrigerated pie crust
3 oz shredded reduced fat Monterey Jack Cheese
   (3/4 cup)
3 oz shredded reduced fat Cheddar Cheese (3/4 cup)
1 cup frozen corn, thawed
2 oz sliced ripe olives (1/2 cup)
1/2 cup sliced green onions
1 cup evaporated skim milk
1 cup Thick & Chunky salsa
4 eggs or equivalent in egg substitute
4 Tablespoons fat free sour cream
   (15 calories per Tablespoon)

Preheat oven to 425 degrees. Bake pie crust for 10 minutes or until lightly browned. Remove from oven and sprinkle cheeses over bottom of crust. Layer corn, olives and onions over cheese. In a small bowl combine milk, 1/2 cup salsa and eggs. Beat well with wire whisk. Pour over mixture in pie crust. Cover edge of crust with strip of foil. Bake for 15 minutes. Lower heat to 350 degrees and bake another 30 minutes or until knife inserted in center comes out clean. Cool 10 minutes before serving. Garnish each serving with 1/2 Tablespoon sour cream and 1 Tablespoon salsa.

HINT: If you can't find reduced fat Monterey Jack cheese, use all reduced fat Cheddar cheese.

Serves 8
Each serving equals:
HE:1 1/2 Pr (1/2 limited),3/4 Br,1/4 SM,1/3 Ve,1/4 Fa,
   1/2 Sl, 18 OC
282 calories, 15 gr Fa, 15 gr Pr, 23 gr Ca, 544 mg So
Diabetic: 1 1/2 Mt, 1 1/2 Fa, 1 St, 1 Ve

Bill wrote me, "real men DO eat quiche if it's Mexicali Quiche"

HEALTHY JO'S

6 hamburger buns (80 calories each)
16 oz ground turkey or beef (90% lean)
1/2 cup chopped onions
1 cup tomato sauce
1/2 cup chunky salsa
Brown sugar substitute to equal
   1 Tablespoon brown sugar

In large skillet sprayed with olive flavored cooking spray, brown meat and onion. Add tomato sauce, salsa and brown sugar substitute. Lower heat and simmer 15-20 minutes. Serve on hamburger buns.

Serves 6 (1/3 cup)
Each serving equals:
HE: 2 Pr, 1 Br, 1 Ve, 1 OC
209 calories, 7 gr Fa, 17 gr Pr, 19 gr Ca, 567 mg So
Diabetic: 2 Mt, 1 St, 1 Ve

My version of the old standby.

SKILLETBURGERS

6 hamburger buns (80 calories each)
16 oz ground turkey or beef (90% lean)
1 cup chopped onion
1 cup chopped celery
1 cup tomato sauce
1/8 teaspoon lemon pepper
1/2 teaspoon chili powder
1/2 teaspoon Worcestershire sauce

In skillet sprayed with cooking spray, brown meat, onion and celery. Add tomato sauce, lemon pepper, chili powder and Worcestershire sauce. Stir to blend. Lower heat and simmer uncovered about 30 minutes, stirring occasionally. Serve on hamburger buns.

Serves 6 (1/2 cup)
Each serving equals:
HE: 2 Pr, 1 1/3 Ve, 1 Br
219 calories, 7 gr Fa, 17 gr Pr, 21 gr Ca, 511 mg So
Diabetic: 2 Mt, 1 St, 1 Ve

James *really enjoyed these. He commented more than once, he enjoyed the celery in it.*

SKILLET HAMBURGER STROGANOFF

8 oz ground turkey or beef (90% lean)

1/2 cup chopped onion

1 can Campbell's Healthy Request Cream of
    Mushroom soup

1/2 cup canned sliced mushrooms, drained

1/4 teaspoon pepper

2 cups cooked noodles

1/4 cup fat free sour cream (15 Calories per Tablespoon)

1/2 teaspoon diced parsley

In large skillet sprayed with cooking spray, brown meat and onion. Add soup, mushrooms, pepper and noodles. Stir well to combine. Simmer 10 minutes. Remove from heat. Stir in sour cream and parsley. Serve at once.

Serves 4
Each serving equals:
HE: 1 1/2 Pr, 1 Br, 1/2 Ve, 1/2 Sl, 16 OC
249 calories, 7 gr Fa, 16 gr Pr, 30 gr Ca, 516 mg So
Diabetic: 1 1/2 Mt, 2 St

A quick version of a longtime favorite.

ITALIAN SHEPHERD'S PIE

8 oz ground turkey or beef (90% lean)
1/4 cup chopped onions
1 3/4 cups Italian stewed tomatoes with juice
2 cups frozen green beans
1 3/4 cups water
3 oz instant potato flakes (1 1/3 cups)
1/3 cup nonfat dry milk powder
3/4 oz grated Parmesan cheese (1/4 cup)
1/2 teaspoon Italian seasoning
3/4 oz shredded reduced fat Mozzarella cheese
   (3 Tablespoons)

Preheat oven to 350 degrees. In large skillet sprayed with olive flavored cooking spray, brown meat and onion. Add stewed tomatoes and green beans. Lower heat. Simmer. Meanwhile bring water to a boil in a medium saucepan. Remove from heat. Stir in potato flakes, nonfat dry milk powder, Parmesan cheese and Italian seasoning. Mix with fork until fluffy. Add mozzarella cheese to meat mixture. Stir until cheese melts. Pour meat mixture into 8x8 baking dish sprayed with olive flavored cooking spray. Evenly divide potato mixture into 4 equal mounds on top of meat mixture. Bake 15-20 minutes. Cool 5 minutes before serving.

Serves 4
Each serving equals:
HE: 2 Pr, 2 Ve, 1 Br, 1/4 SM
265 calories, 7 gr Fa, 19 gr Pr, 32 gr Ca, 520 mg So
Diabetic: 2 Mt, 2 Ve, 1 1/2 St

A taste sensation to be enjoyed over and over.

RUNZA'S

8 frozen yeast dinner rolls (80 calories per roll or less)
8 oz ground turkey or beef (90% lean)
1/4 cup chopped onion
1 cup shredded cole slaw mix
1 Tablespoon Sloppy Joe seasoning mix
1/2 teaspoon salt
1/8 teaspoon pepper

Spray medium cookie sheet with butter flavored cooking spray. Evenly space frozen rolls on sheet. Cover with cloth and let thaw and rise. In medium skillet sprayed with butter flavored cooking spray, cook at medium high temperature meat, onion, cole slaw mix, Sloppy Joe seasoning mix, salt and pepper. Cook 10-12 minutes, stirring frequently. Cool. When rolls have risen, flatten one at a time and place a generous tablespoon of filling in center of each. Gently cover filling and form into roll. Place seam side down on cookie sheet. When done forming all rolls, quickly spray tops with butter flavored cooking spray. Cover with cloth again and let rolls rest for 10-15 minutes. Bake at 400 degrees for 15-18 minutes or until golden brown. Remove from oven and spray again with butter flavored cooking spray. Place sheet on wire rack and let cool slightly before serving.

HINT: 1) 1/4 cup shredded carrots and 3/4 cup shredded cabbage can be used in place of cole slaw mix

2) Freezes well

Serves 8
Each serving equals:
HE: 1 Br, 3/4 Pr, 1/3 Ve
121 calories, 3 gr Fa, 8 gr Pr, 15 gr Ca, 262 mg So
Diabetic: 1 St, 1 Mt

Janice, *a subscriber tried these and dropped me a note stating her husband had said if she wanted to open a runza stand in town, she could make her fortune.*

FIESTA BAKE

8 oz ground turkey or beef (90% lean)
1/2 cup chopped onion
1/4 cup chopped green bell pepper
1/2 cup canned sliced mushrooms, drained
1 cup frozen corn
1 cup tomato sauce
1 Tablespoon chili seasoning mix
3/4 cup Bisquick Reduced Fat baking mix
3/4 cup chunky salsa
1 1/2 oz shredded reduced fat Cheddar cheese (1/3 cup)

Preheat oven to 350 degrees. In large skillet sprayed with olive flavored cooking spray, brown meat, onion and green pepper. Add mushrooms, corn, tomato sauce and chili seasoning mix. Stir well to blend. Pour into 8x8 baking dish sprayed with olive flavored cooking spray. In medium bowl combine biscuit baking mix and salsa. Add cheese; mix well. Spread evenly over meat mixture. Bake 25-30 minutes.

Serves 6
Each serving equals:
HE: 1 1/3 Pr, 1 1/3 Ve, 1 Br
282 calories, 9 gr Fa, 19 gr Pr, 32 gr Ca, 1056 mg So
Diabetic: 2 Mt, 1 Ve, 1 1/2 St

This was a "major league hit" when I served this to the ladies helping with the newsletter.

CHILI SPAGHETTI

8 oz ground turkey or beef (90% lean)
1/2 cup chopped onion
1/2 cup chopped green pepper
1 3/4 cups tomato sauce with tomato bits
10 oz canned kidney beans, rinsed and drained
1/8 teaspoon pepper
2 teaspoons chili powder
3 cups cooked spaghetti
2 1/4 oz shredded reduced fat Monterey Jack and
   Colby Cheese or Cheddar cheese (full 1/2 cup)

In skillet sprayed with butter flavored cooking spray, saute meat, onions and green pepper. Add tomato sauce, kidney beans, pepper and chili powder. Simmer for 10-15 minutes. Evenly divide spaghetti; top with chili sauce. Evenly garnish each serving with shredded cheese.

HINT: A 16 oz can of beans is 10 oz drained weight.

Serves 6
Each serving equals:
HE: 2 1/3 Pr, 1 1/2 Ve, 1 Br
289 calories, 7 gr Fa, 19 gr Pr, 38 gr Ca, 523 mg So
Diabetic: 2 Mt, 2 St, 1 Ve

Try it, you may actually like it. My family did.

CAVATINI

2 cups cooked pasta, any variety or varieties
8 oz Turkey Italian sausage (90% lean)
1 cup chopped green pepper
1 cup chopped onion
1 cup tomato paste
1 cup water
1/2 cup canned sliced mushrooms, drained
2 oz black olives, sliced (1/2 cup)
1 Tablespoon pizza seasoning
3 oz shredded reduced fat Cheddar cheese (3/4 cup)
3 oz shredded reduced fat Mozzarella cheese (3/4 cup)

Preheat oven to 350 degrees. In large skillet sprayed with olive flavored cooking spray, brown sausage with green pepper and onion. Add tomato paste, water, mushrooms, olives, pizza seasoning, pasta and cheddar cheese. Spray an 8x8 baking dish with olive flavored cooking spray. Place pasta mixture in dish. Cover. Bake 20-30 minutes. Sprinkle mozzarella cheese on top and bake until cheese melts, about 5-6 minutes.

HINT: 1) 1 3/4 cups tomato sauce with tomato bits can be used in place of tomato paste and water.

2) If you can't find Turkey Italian sausage, use ground turkey or beef, 1 teaspoon Italian seasoning and 1/2 teaspoon ground sage

Serves 6
Each serving equals:
HE: 2 1/3 Pr, 1 1/2 Ve, 3/4 Br, 1/3 Fa
311 calories, 13 gr Fa, 22 gr Pr, 27 gr Ca, 931 mg So
Diabetic: 2 Mt, 2 Ve, 1 St, 1/2 Fa

*When my friend **Gayle** asked me to make over a family favorite, it quickly became a favorite of families all over.*

'QUICK' LASAGNA CASSEROLE

8 oz ground turkey or beef (90% lean)
3/4 cup chopped onion
1 3/4 cups Italian stewed tomatoes with juice
1 cup tomato sauce
1/2 teaspoon minced garlic
1 1/3 cups low fat cottage cheese
1 egg or equivalent in egg substitute
3 cups cooked mini lasagna macaroni
3/4 oz grated Parmesan cheese (1/4 cup)
2 1/4 oz shredded reduced fat Mozzarella cheese
   (full 1/2 cup)

Preheat oven to 375 degrees. In large skillet sprayed with olive flavored cooking spray, brown meat and onion. Add Italian stewed tomatoes, tomato sauce and minced garlic. Simmer 10-15 minutes. In blender combine cottage cheese and egg. Puree' until smooth. Spray an 8x8 baking dish with olive flavored cooking spray. Spread 3/4 cup meat sauce on bottom of casserole. Layer half of cooked mini lasagna macaroni over sauce. Pour half of cottage cheese mixture over lasagna macaroni. Pour half of meat sauce over top. Sprinkle with half of Parmesan and mozzarella cheese. Repeat layers. Bake 35-40 minutes. Let stand 10 minutes before cutting.

Serves 6
Each serving equals:
HE:2 1/2 Pr, 1 1/2 Ve, 1 Br
289 Calories, 8 gr Fa, 23 gr Pr, 31 gr Ca, 809 mg So
Diabetic: 2 1/2 Mt, 2 Ve, 1 St

*This recipe was created when a caller to our radio program requested a fast way to prepare lasagna. My daughter-in-law **PAM**, a true lasagna lover, really enjoyed this version.*

MEXICAN LASAGNA

8 oz ground turkey or beef (90% lean)

3/4 cup onion, chopped

1 3/4 cups Mexican stewed tomatoes,
    coarsely chopped with juice

1 cup tomato sauce

1 (1 1/2 oz) pkg Taco seasoning mix

4 (6 inch) corn tortillas

1 1/2 oz shredded reduced fat Cheddar cheese (1/3 cup)

Preheat oven to 350 degrees. In large skillet sprayed with cooking spray, brown meat and onion. Add stewed tomatoes and tomato sauce. Mix in taco seasoning. Place a thin layer of meat mixture on bottom of 8x8 baking dish sprayed with olive flavored cooking spray. Top with 2 tortillas. Turn to fit. Spread half of remaining sauce over top. Sprinkle half of cheese over sauce. Layer 2 more tortillas over cheese. Turn to fit. Spread remaining sauce over tortillas. Sprinkle remaining cheese over top. Bake uncovered for 30 minutes.

Serves 4
Each serving equals:
HE: 2 1/4 Ve, 2 Pr, 1 Br
212 calories, 7 gr Fa, 16 gr Pr, 22 gr Ca, 818 mg So
Diabetic: 2 Ve, 2 Mt, 1 St

*My son **James** doesn't care for cottage cheese, so I came up with a version with a Mexican flavor for him. He loved it.*

SOUTH OF THE BORDER LASAGNA

8 oz ground turkey or beef (90% lean)
1/2 cup chopped onion
1/2 cup chopped green pepper
1 3/4 cups tomato sauce with tomato bits
1/2 cup chunky salsa
1/2 teaspoon minced garlic
2 cups cooked mini lasagna macaroni
1 cup frozen whole kernel corn
3 oz shredded reduced fat Cheddar cheese (3/4 cup)
1 teaspoon dried parsley or 1 Tablespoon fresh
   chopped parsley or cilrento

Preheat oven to 375 degrees. In large skillet sprayed with olive flavored cooking spray, brown meat, onion and green pepper. Add tomato sauce, chunky salsa and minced garlic. Simmer 10-15 minutes. Spray an 8x8 baking dish with olive flavored cooking spray. Spread 3/4 cup meat sauce in bottom of casserole. Layer 1 cup cooked mini lasagna macaroni over sauce. Sprinkle 1/2 cup corn over top. Pour half of remaining meat sauce over corn. Top with half of cheddar cheese. Repeat layers. Sprinkle parsley over top. Bake 30-35 minutes. Let stand 10 minutes before cutting.

Serves 6
Each serving equals:
HE: 1 2/3 Pr, 1 2/3 Ve, 1 Br
225 calories, 7 gr Fa, 15 gr Pr, 26 gr Ca, 631 mg So
Diabetic: 1 1/2 Mt, 2 Ve, 1 St

*My truck drivin' man, **Cliff** loves Mexican inspired foods. This one wasn't a disappointment to him.*

TEXAS HASH

8 oz ground turkey or beef (90% lean)
3/4 cup diced onion
1/2 cup diced green pepper
1 3/4 cups Mexican style stewed tomatoes with juice
1 cup cooked rice
1 teaspoon chili powder
1/8 teaspoon pepper

In large skillet sprayed with cooking spray, brown meat, onion and green pepper. Add stewed tomatoes, cooked rice, chili powder and pepper. Lower heat and simmer 10-15 minutes, stirring occasionally.

Serves 4
Each serving equals:
HE: 1 1/2 Pr, 1 1/2 Ve, 1/2 Br
169 calories, 5 gr Fa, 12 gr Pr, 19 gr Ca, 339 mg So
Diabetic: 1 Ve, 1 1/2 Mt, 1 St

Who said hash could only be corned beef? Sink your teeth into this version.

TD CHOP SUEY

8 oz ground turkey or beef (90% lean)
1 cup chopped onion
2 cups chopped celery
1 cup canned bean sprouts, drained (optional)
1/2 cup canned sliced mushrooms, drained
1 3/4 cups canned beef broth
2 Tablespoons cornstarch
2 Tablespoons reduced sodium soy sauce
2 cups hot cooked rice

In large skillet sprayed with cooking spray, saute meat, onions and celery until meat is browned. Add bean sprouts and mushrooms. In covered jar combine beef broth and cornstarch. Add to meat mixture. Cook 10 minutes stirring until mixture starts to thicken. Add soy sauce. Stir and serve over hot rice.

Serves 4
Each serving equals:
HE: 2 1/4 Ve, 1 1/2 Pr, 1 Br, 24 OC
227 calories, 6 gr Fa, 14 gr Pr, 29 gr Ca, 668 mg So
Diabetic: 1 St, 1 1/2 Mt, 2 Ve

*This is named for my son **TOM** because he really loved taste testing it.*

MEXICAN "SWISS" STEAK

1 Tablespoon flour
1 Tablespoon chili seasoning mix
4 (4 oz) lean minute beef steaks
1 3/4 cups tomato sauce with tomato bits
1/2 cup chunky salsa

In flat dish combine flour and chili seasoning mix. Gently coat steaks. Spray a large skillet with olive flavored cooking spray. Brown steaks on both sides over medium heat. Combine tomato sauce and salsa. Pour over steaks. Lower heat. Cover and simmer 20-30 minutes. "Gravy" is good over rice, potatoes or pasta.

Serves 4
Each serving equals:
HE: 3 Pr, 2 Ve, 8 OC
245 calories, 10 gr Fa, 28 gr Pr, 10 gr Ca, 764 mg So
Diabetic: 3 Mt, 2 Ve

I leave the degree of spicyness of the salsa to you. If you're a wimp like me, use mild. But, if you love the feel of smoke coming out your ears the way **Cliff** *does, then go for the extra hot!*

PIZZA MINUTE STEAKS

4 (4 oz) lean minute beef steaks
1 Tablespoon flour
1 1/2 teaspoons Italian seasoning
1 Tablespoon Sprinkle Sweet
1 3/4 cups tomato sauce with tomato bits
1/2 cup chopped onion
1/2 cup chopped green pepper
1/2 cup canned sliced mushrooms, drained
3/4 oz shredded reduced fat Mozzarella cheese
   (3 Tablespoons)

In flat dish combine flour and 1 teaspoon Italian seasoning. Gently coat steaks. Spray a large skillet with olive flavored cooking spray. Brown steaks on both sides over medium heat. Add Sprinkle Sweet and 1/2 teaspoon Italian seasoning to tomato sauce. Pour over browned meat. Add onion, green pepper and sliced mushrooms. Lower heat. Cover and simmer 25-30 minutes, stirring occasionally. Just before serving sprinkle Mozzarella cheese over steaks. Sauce good served with pasta, rice or potatoes.

Serves 4
Each serving equals:
HE: 3 1/4 Pr, 2 1/2 Ve, 9 OC
273 Calories, 11 gr Fa, 31 gr Pr, 13 gr Ca, 794 mg So
Diabetic: 3 Mt, 2 Ve

Both tummy warming and aroma pleasing.

HAMBURGER MILK GRAVY WITH NOODLES

8 oz ground turkey or beef (90% lean)
2 cups skim milk
3 Tablespoons flour
1/2 cup canned sliced mushrooms, drained
1/2 cup frozen peas
1 teaspoon parsley flakes
1/8 teaspoon pepper
1 1/2 cups cooked noodles

In large skillet sprayed with cooking spray, brown meat. In covered jar combine milk and flour. Pour into meat mixture. Add mushrooms, peas, parsley flakes and pepper. Stir until mixture starts to thicken. Add noodles; mix well. Continue cooking until gravy is thick.

Serves 4
Each serving equals:
HE: 1 1/2 Pr, 1 1/4 Br, 1/2 SM, 1/4 Ve
249 calories, 6 gr Fa, 19 gr Pr, 29 gr Ca, 262 mg So
Diabetic: 1 1/2 Mt, 1 1/2 St, 1/2 SM

*My son **Tom** just loves hamburger milk gravy and in just about any variation. I know beyond a doubt, before he gives a girl an engagement ring, she'll have to pass the hamburger milk gravy test! He said to tell you he loves this version.*

TOMMY'S HAMBURGER MILK GRAVY CASSEROLE

1 1/2 cups evaporated skim milk
2 cups water
4 1/2 oz instant potato flakes (2 cups)
1/2 cup sliced canned mushrooms, drained
8 oz ground turkey or beef (90% lean)
1 Tablespoon flour

Preheat oven to 350 degrees. In large saucepan bring water and 1/2 cup evaporated skim milk to a boil. Add potato flakes. Stir with fork until fluffy. Add mushrooms. Place evenly in 8x8 baking dish sprayed with butter flavored cooking spray. Brown meat. In covered jar combine 1 cup evaporated skim milk and 1 Tablespoon flour. Add to browned meat. Stir until sauce starts to thicken, mixing well. Pour evenly over potatoes. Bake 15-20 minutes. Cool 5 minutes before cutting.

(Serves 4)
Each serving equals:
HE: 1 1/2 Br, 1 1/2 Pr, 3/4 SM, 1/4 Ve, 8 OC
286 calories, 5 gr Fa, 21 gr Pr, 40 Ca, 318 mg So
Diabetic: 1 1/2 St, 1 1/2 Mt, 1 SM

*Another one created while **Tom** was home from college.*

ZUCCHINI STROGANOFF

8 oz ground turkey or beef (90% lean)
1/2 cup chopped onion
1 1/2 cups evaporated skim milk
3 Tablespoons flour
1/2 cup canned sliced mushrooms, drained
2 cups sliced zucchini
1/2 teaspoon dried basil
1 1/2 cups cooked noodles
3/4 cup plain fat free yogurt

In large skillet sprayed with cooking spray, brown meat and onion. In covered jar combine evaporated skim milk and flour. Add to browned meat mixture. Stir well to blend. Add mushrooms, zucchini and basil. Cover; lower heat and simmer 10-15 minutes, stirring occasionally. Add cooked noodles and yogurt. Mix well and cook until warmed through.

Serves 4
Each serving equals:
HE: 1 1/2 Ve, 1 1/2 Pr, 1 SM, 1 Br
310 calories, 6 gr Fa, 25 gr Pr, 39 gr Ca, 325 mg So
Diabetic: 1 1/2 Mt, 1 Ve, 1 SM, 1 St

*My son **Tom** claimed he didn't like zucchini. But, all I can say is when I fixed this, he asked for seconds and later that evening finished the leftovers for his supper... Who do you think he's kidding?*

HAWAIIAN PORK

4 (4 oz) lean pork cube steaks or tenderloins
1 cup tomato sauce
1 cup crushed pineapple, packed in its own juice,
    undrained
1 teaspoon lemon juice
Brown sugar substitute to equal 3 Tablespoons
1/4 teaspoon minced garlic
1/8 teaspoon lemon pepper

In skillet sprayed with cooking spray, brown pork steaks over medium heat. In medium bowl combine tomato sauce, undrained pineapple, lemon juice, brown sugar substitute, minced garlic and lemon pepper. Pour sauce over meat. Cover. Lower heat and simmer 15 minutes.

Serves 4
Each serving equals:
HE: 3 Pr, 1 Ve, 1/2 Fr, 5 OC
200 calories, 4 gr Fa, 25 gr Pr, 15 gr Ca, 424 mg So
Diabetic: 3 Mt, 1 Fr

A tasty way to enjoy a trip to Hawaii without leaving home.

RANCHERO PORK BAKE

4 (4 oz) lean pork cutlets or tenderloins
1 Tablespoon flour
1 Tablespoon chili seasoning mix
1/2 cup chopped onion
1/2 cup chopped green pepper
10 oz canned red kidney beans, rinsed and drained
1 cup chunky salsa

Preheat oven to 350 degrees. In small bowl combine flour and chili seasoning mix. Place in shallow dish and evenly coat pork cutlets. Spray large skillet with olive flavored cooking spray. When skillet is hot, brown cutlets on both sides. Meanwhile, in medium skillet sprayed with olive flavored cooking spray, saute onions and green pepper until vegetables are tender. Add drained kidney beans and salsa. Mix well. Pour into 8x8 baking dish. Place browned pork cutlets on top of bean mixture. Cover with aluminum foil and bake 35 minutes. Uncover and bake 10 minutes more.

HINT: A 16 oz can of kidney beans is 10 oz drained weight.

Serves 4
Each serving equals:
HE: 3 Pr, 1 1/4 Br, 1 Ve, 8 OC
259 calories,5 gr Fa, 31 gr Pr, 23 gr Ca, 283 mg So
Diabetic: 4 Mt, 1 1/2 St

This if for all my cowboy wanabe's. Maybe it will work for yours as well.

PORK ALA KING

8 oz cooked lean roast pork, cubed
3 Tablespoons flour
1 1/2 cups evaporated skim milk
1/2 cup canned button mushrooms, drained
2 Tablespoons pimento, diced and drained
1 cup frozen peas, thawed
1/4 teaspoon thyme
1/2 teaspoon lemon pepper

In covered jar combine flour and evaporated skim milk. Pour into medium saucepan sprayed with butter flavored cooking spray. Cook over medium heat, stirring constantly until thickened. Stir in mushrooms, pimento, peas, thyme and lemon pepper. Gently stir in pork and stir until pork is warmed through. Good served over noodles, rice or toast.

Serves 4
Each serving equals:
HE: 2 Pr, 3/4 Br, 3/4 SM
270 calories, 8 gr Fa, 26 gr Pr, 22 gr Ca, 298 mg So
Diabetic: 2 Mt, 1 St, 1 SM

Cindy *gave me a family favorite to make over. This is the final result.*

JERRY'S WESTERN CHICKEN

1 packet Lipton's onion-mushroom soup mix
16 oz skinless chicken breasts, split into 4 servings
1/4 cup barbecue sauce
1/2 cup fat free Western French Dressing
   (20 calories per Tablespoon)

Spray microwavable dish with cooking spray. Sprinkle dry soup mix over bottom of dish. Place chicken in dish, meat side down. Combine barbecue sauce and Western Dressing. Pour over chicken breasts. Microwave on high for 8 minutes, turning dish after 4 minutes. Turn chicken meat side up. Stir sauce and soup mix together. Baste chicken. Microwave another 4-6 minutes or until chicken is cooked through.

Serves 4
Each serving equals:
HE: 3 Pr, 1 Sl, 27 OC
252 calories, 11 gr Fa, 24 gr Pr, 11 gr Ca, 598 mg So
Diabetic: 3 Mt, 1 St

You guessed it. **Jerry,** *the husband of one of my subscribers created and shares this recipe with us.*

"GUSSIED UP" CHICKEN FETTUCCINE

4 oz diced cooked chicken breast
1 1/2 oz grated Parmesan cheese (1/2 cup)
2 teaspoons reduced calorie margarine
1/4 cup evaporated skim milk
1 1/2 cups cooked fettuccine
1/2 teaspoon dried basil or 1 Tablespoon fresh, chopped
1 cup broccoli, cooked tender crisp
1 medium tomato, diced

In large bowl combine chicken, cheese, margarine, evaporated skim milk and hot drained fettuccine. Add basil, broccoli and tomato. Mix gently to combine. Serve at once.

Serves 2
Each serving equals:
HE: 3 Pr, 1 1/2 Br, 1 1/4 Ve, 1/4 Fa, 1/4 SM
386 calories, 10 gr Fa, 35 gr Pr, 40 gr Ca, 454 mg So
Diabetic: 4 Mt, 2 St, 1 Ve

*When **Cliff** ordered this in a restaurant, I ate it with my eyes then went home and created this the next day. He loved my version.*

CHICKEN SALAD PIE

1 purchased 9" unbaked refrigerated pie crust
9 oz diced cooked chicken breast
3 oz shredded reduced fat Cheddar cheese (3/4 cup)
1 cup diced celery
1 cup crushed pineapple, packed in its own juice, drained
1 oz chopped walnuts (1/4 cup)
2/3 cup reduced calorie whipped topping
    (8 calories per Tablespoon)
2/3 cup fat free mayonnaise (8 calories per Tablespoon)
1/2 teaspoon lemon pepper

Bake pie crust according to package directions. Cool on wire rack. In large mixing bowl combine chicken, 1/2 cup cheese, celery, pineapple, walnuts, 1/3 cup whipped topping, 1/3 cup mayonnaise and lemon pepper. Spread in cooled pie crust. In small bowl combine 1/3 cup mayonnaise and 1/3 cup whipped topping. Spread evenly over filling. Sprinkle remaining 1/4 cup cheese over top. Chill until ready to serve.

Serves 8
Each serving equals:
HE: 1 3/4 Pr, 1/2 Br, 1/4 Ve, 1/4 Fr, 1/4 Fa, 1/2 Sl, 31 OC
272 calories, 13 gr Fa, 16 gr Pr, 23 gr Ca, 422 mg So
Diabetic: 1 1/2 Mt, 1 1/2 Fa, 1 St, 1/2 Fr

When I had a refrigerated pie crust fast approaching the expiration date, this salad pie was created. It's perfect for a hot summer supper.

SOUTHWESTERN CHICKEN PASTA SALAD

2 cups cooked Rotini macaroni
4 oz diced cooked chicken breast
1 1/2 oz shredded reduced fat Cheddar cheese (1/3 cup)
1/3 cup fat free mayonnaise (8 calories per Tablespoon)
1 teaspoon lime juice
2 teaspoons chili seasoning mix

In large bowl combine Rotini macaroni, chicken and cheese. In small bowl combine mayonnaise, lime juice and chili seasoning mix. Blend into Rotini mixture. Cover and chill.

Serves 4   (1 cup)
Each serving equals:
HE: 1 1/2 Pr, 1 Br, 11 OC
186 calories, 3 gr Fa, 15 gr Pr, 24 gr Ca, 269 mg So
Diabetic: 1 1/2 Mt, 1 1/2 St

An enjoyable way to prepare a main dish salad.

CHEESY ASPARAGUS BAKE

1 lb fresh asparagus, cut into 1" pieces
2 Tablespoons flour
1/4 teaspoon salt
1/4 teaspoon dry mustard
1/8 teaspoon pepper
1 cup skim milk
3 oz shredded reduced fat Cheddar cheese (3/4 cup)
3/4 oz dry bread crumbs (3 Tablespoons)
1 oz chopped cashews (1/4 cup)

Cook asparagus in water until crisp tender. Place in 8x8 baking dish. In covered jar combine flour, salt, dry mustard, pepper and milk. Pour into medium saucepan sprayed with butter flavored cooking spray. Cook over medium heat until sauce is thick. Layer cheese on top of asparagus. Pour sauce over cheese. In small bowl combine bread crumbs and cashews. Sprinkle crumb mixture over top of cheese. Quickly spray top with butter flavored cooking spray. Bake uncovered in 350 degree oven 20-30 minutes.

Serves 4
Each serving equals:
HE: 1 1/4 Pr, 1 Ve, 1/2 Fa, 1/4 SM, 1/4 Br, 15 OC
195 calories, 8 gr Fa, 14 gr Pr, 17 gr Ca, 439 mg So
Diabetic: 2 Ve, 1 Mt, 1 Fa

Keslee *said this had "uptown taste". I think you will agree.*

ASPARAGUS AND HAM IN CHEESE SAUCE

24 cooked asparagus spears
8 (1 oz) slices cooked ham (90% lean)
1 Tablespoon flour
1/2 cup evaporated skim milk
1/8 teaspoon lemon pepper
1 1/2 oz shredded reduced fat Swiss cheese (1/3 cup)

Preheat oven to 375 degrees. Wrap 3 asparagus spears in each ham slice. Place in 8x8 baking dish. In covered jar combine flour, evaporated skim milk and lemon pepper. Pour into saucepan sprayed with butter flavored cooking spray. Cook over low heat, stirring constantly until thickened. Add Swiss cheese. Stir to melt. Pour over ham rolls. Bake for 15 minutes.

HINT: Go to the Deli and ask them to slice some extra lean ham into 8 (1 oz) slices. It is much easier on your nerves and fingers.

Serves 4 (2 rolls each)
Each serving equals:
HE: 2 1/2 Pr, 1 Ve, 1/4 SM, 8 OC
152 calories, 5 gr Fa, 16 gr Pr, 11 gr Ca, 683 mg So
Diabetic: 2 Mt, 1 1/2 Ve

A pleasant way to enjoy traditional ingredients.

HAM AND ASPARAGUS AU GRATIN

3 cups chopped asparagus
10 oz sliced raw potatoes (2 cups)
1/2 cup chopped onion
5 oz diced ham (90% lean)
1 1/2 cups evaporated skim milk
3 Tablespoons flour
2 1/4 oz shredded reduced fat Cheddar cheese
    (full 1/2 cup)
3/4 oz dry bread crumbs (3 Tablespoons)

Mix asparagus and potatoes together and place in 8x8 baking dish. Add 3 Tablespoons water, cover and microwave on high for 6-7 minutes or until crisp-tender. Meanwhile, spray large skillet with butter flavored cooking spray. Saute onions over medium heat until almost tender. Add diced ham. In covered jar combine evaporated skim milk and flour. Add to onion-ham mixture. Stir until sauce starts to thicken. Add shredded cheese. Cook until cheese melts, stirring constantly. Drain potatoes and asparagus, if needed. Return to 8x8 dish. Pour sauce mixture over top and mix well to blend. Microwave on medium for 10 minutes. Sprinkle bread crumbs over top. Quickly spray with butter flavored cooking spray and microwave on high for 60 seconds.

HINT: Dubuque 97% fat free ham works great.

Serves 4
Each serving equals:
HE: 2 Pr, 1 3/4 Ve, 1 Br, 3/4 SM
289 calories, 5 gr Fa, 23 gr Pr, 38 gr Ca, 587 mg So
Diabetic: 2 Mt, 2 Ve, 1 St, 1 SM

*My friend **JoAnn** shares this tasty dish with us.*

BROCCOLI-PARMESAN WITH NOODLES

1 (10 oz) pkg frozen broccoli, chopped
1/2 cup chopped onion
2 cups fresh mushrooms, sliced
1/2 teaspoon lemon pepper
1 1/2 oz grated Parmesan cheese (1/2 cup)
2 cups cooked noodles

In medium saucepan cook broccoli in water until tender; drain. Meanwhile saute onions and mushrooms in skillet sprayed with butter flavored cooking spray. Add drained broccoli and lemon pepper. Continue cooking for about 5 minutes. Remove from heat. Stir in Parmesan cheese. Serve over noodles.

Serves 4
Each serving equals:
HE: 2 1/4 Ve, 1 Br, 1/2 Pr
191 calories, 5 gr Fa, 11 gr Pr, 27 gr Ca, 255 mg So
Diabetic; 2 Ve, 1 St, 1 Mt

*My son **TOM** loved this. He wanted to take the recipe back with him to college.*

BROCCOLI AND HAM SAUCE
WITH CHEESE BISCUITS

3 cups frozen cut broccoli
1 1/2 cups evaporated skim milk
3 Tablespoons flour
1 Tablespoon instant minced onion
1 Tablespoon Worcestershire sauce
5 oz diced ham (90% lean)

In medium saucepan cook frozen broccoli in water; drain. In covered jar combine evaporated skim milk and flour. In same saucepan sprayed with butter flavored cooking spray, combine milk mixture, onion flakes and Worcestershire sauce. Cook over medium heat, stirring often until sauce starts to thicken. Add diced ham and drained broccoli. Heat through. Serve over hot cheese biscuits.

Cheese Biscuits

1 cup + 2 Tablespoons Bisquick Reduced Fat Baking mix
1 1/2 oz shredded reduced fat Cheddar cheese (1/3 cup)
1/3 cup nonfat dry milk powder
1/2 cup water

In medium mixing bowl combine baking mix, dry milk powder and cheese. Add water. Mix well. Drop evenly on sprayed baking sheet. Bake at 425 degrees for 8-10 minutes.

Serves 4
Each serving equals:
HE: 1 3/4 Br, 1 3/4 Pr, 1 1/2 Ve, 1 SM
328 calories, 6 gr Fa, 24 gr Pr, 46 gr Ca, 955 mg So
Diabetic: 1 1/2 St, 1 1/2 Mt, 1 1/2 Ve, 1 SM

The cheese biscuits are a snap to make. And, they blend so well with the broccoli and ham sauce.

HAM AND PEA STUFFED TOMATOES

1/4 cup fat free mayonnaise (8 calories per Tablespoon)
1/2 teaspoon prepared mustard
1/8 teaspoon pepper
1 cup frozen peas, thawed
5 oz diced ham (90% lean)
2 Tablespoons green onion, sliced
4 medium tomatoes

In medium bowl combine mayonnaise, mustard and pepper. Add peas, diced ham and onion. Cover and chill at least 1 hour. Slice top off tomatoes. Scoop out center pulp and seeds. Chill tomatoes until ready to serve. Just before serving spoon pea-ham salad into tomatoes. Serve on lettuce greens.

Serves 4
Each serving equals:
HE: 1 1/4 Pr, 1 Ve, 1/2 Br, 8 OC
125 calories, 4 gr Fa, 9 gr Pr, 15 gr Ca, 472 mg So
Diabetic: 1 Mt, 1/2 St, 1 Ve

A very refreshing main dish for a hot summer night.

KARLA'S LAST MINUTE CASSEROLE

3 ounces uncooked Rotini noodles (full 1 cup)
2 cups frozen California Blend Vegetables
4 oz diced ham (90% lean)
1 can Campbell's Healthy Request Cream of
    Mushroom Soup
3 oz shredded reduced fat Cheddar cheese (3/4 cup)
1/8 teaspoon pepper
1/2 teaspoon dried parsley

In medium saucepan cook noodles and vegetables in
water. Drain. Add diced ham. Combine soup, cheese,
pepper and parsley. Add to noodle mixture. Pour into an
8x8 baking dish and bake 20 minutes at 350 degrees.

Serves 4
Each serving equals:
HE: 2 Pr, 1 Br, 1 Ve, 1/2 Sl, 1 OC
217 calories, 8 gr Fa, 15 gr Pr, 21 gr Ca, 737 mg So
Diabetic: 2 Mt, 1 1/2 St, 1 Ve

Karla *is a friend I've made through the newsletter. She
shares a recipe she created when she was running late
one night.*

CORDON BLEU RICE DISH

6 oz cooked turkey, cut into strips
3 oz cooked ham (90% lean), cut into strips
1 cup Campbells Healthy Request canned chicken broth
1/2 cup evaporated skim milk
1 Tablespoon flour
2 cups frozen cut green beans, thawed
2 Tablespoons Dijon style mustard
3 oz uncooked instant rice (1 cup)
1 1/2 oz shredded reduced fat Swiss cheese (1/3 cup)

In skillet sprayed with butter flavored cooking spray, saute turkey and ham until lightly browned. In covered jar combine broth, evaporated skim milk and flour. Pour over meat. Add green beans and mustard. Bring to a full boil. Stir in rice. Top with shredded cheese. Cover. Remove from heat. Let stand 5 minutes. Fluff with fork before serving.

HINT: Dubuque 97% fat free ham works great.

Serves 4
Each serving equals:
HE: 2 3/4 Pr, 1 Ve, 3/4 Br, 1/4 SM, 12 OC
276 calories, 7 gr Fa, 25 gr Pr, 29 gr Ca, 829 mg So
Diabetic: 2 1/2 Mt, 1 1/2 St, 1 Ve

An elegant (but not too elegant) dish to serve for company.

BAYOU JAMBALAYA

3/4 cup sliced onion
1/2 cup chopped green bell pepper
1 minced clove garlic
2 Tablespoons catsup
1 3/4 cups Cajun stewed tomatoes with juice
1 cup water
3 oz uncooked white rice, not instant (1 cup)
4 oz diced ham (90% lean)
4 oz medium-size shrimp, frozen or canned, rinsed
    and drained

In large skillet sprayed with cooking spray, saute onion, green pepper and garlic until onion is tender. Stir in catsup, tomatoes and water. Add rice and ham. Cover and simmer 20-25 minutes or until rice is tender. Add shrimp and simmer uncovered until shrimp is warmed through, about 2-4 minutes, stirring occasionally.

HINT: Dubuque 97% fat free ham works great.

Serves 4
Each serving equals:
HE: 1 1/2 Pr, 1 1/2 Ve, 3/4 Br, 8 OC
191 calories, 2 gr Fa, 14 gr Pr, 30 gr Ca, 664 mg So
Diabetic: 2 Mt, 2 Ve, 1 St

*This passed my son **TOM'S** taste test.*

CALIFORNIA TUNA BAKE

2 cups cooked garden variety rotini noodles
6 oz tuna, packed in water, drained and flaked
1 cup frozen peas
1 oz sliced pimento stuffed olives (1/4 cup)
2 Tablespoons dried minced onion
1 can Campbell's Healthy Request Cream of
    Mushroom soup
1/3 cup nonfat dry milk powder
4 oz fat free cream cheese, cubed (1/2 cup)
1/4 teaspoon lemon pepper

Preheat oven to 350 degrees. In large bowl combine noodles, tuna, peas, olives and minced onion. Add mushroom soup, dry milk powder, cream cheese and lemon pepper. Mix well to blend. Pour into 8x8 baking dish sprayed with olive flavored cooking spray. Cover. Bake 30 minutes.

Serves 4
Each serving equals:
HE: 1 1/2 Br, 1 1/4 Pr, 1/4 Fa, 1/4 SM, 1/2 Sl, 1 OC
267 calories, 3 gr Fa, 23 gr Pr, 37 gr Ca, 848 mg So
Diabetic: 2 St, 2 Mt

An updated version of the old casserole standby.

MOCK LOBSTER

16 oz frozen haddock
1 teaspoon salt
2 Tablespoons vinegar

Place haddock in large saucepan and just cover with hot water. Add salt and vinegar. Bring to boiling point and boil for 20 minutes. Carefully remove fish from water and place on broiler of oven. Broil 3-5 minutes on each side to dry fish. Serve with lemon juice or hot melted reduced calorie margarine. If using margarine, count accordingly.

Serves 4
Each serving equals:
HE: 1 1/2 Pr
100 calories,less than 1 gr Fa, 21 gr Pr, 0 gr Ca, 610 mg So
Diabetic: 3 Mt

If you have lobster taste, but live within a sardine budget, this may do the trick for you.

GERMAN GOULASH

12 oz Healthy Choice Kielbasa, cut
   into 1" chunks (97% lean)
1 3/4 cups stewed tomatoes with juice
2 cups Bavarian style sauerkraut, drained
15 oz raw potatoes, peeled and cut into chunks (3 cups)
3/4 cup diced onion

Cook Kielbasa and drain. In medium saucepan combine tomatoes, sauerkraut, potatoes, onion and cooked Kielbasa. Bring to a boil; lower heat and simmer until potatoes are done, about 45 minutes.

HINT: If you can't find 97% fat free Kielbasa, use Healthy Choice 97% fat free frankfurters.

Serves 4
Each serving equals:
HE: 2 1/4 Ve, 2 Pr, 3/4 Br
258 calories, 3 gr Fa, 20 gr Pr, 38 gr Ca, 1763 mg So
Diabetic: 2 Mt, 2 Ve, 1 1/2 St

A very tasty way to serve sauerkraut.

CREAMED CHIPPED BEEF

6 oz dried chipped beef (90% lean)
3 Tablespoons flour
2 cups skim milk
4 oz fat free cream cheese
1/8 teaspoon pepper
1/2 teaspoon dried parsley flakes

Shred beef with knife into thin strips. Spray large skillet with butter flavored cooking spray. Add beef. In covered jar combine flour and milk. Pour over beef. Stir to combine. Add cream cheese and stir until cheese melts. Add pepper and parsley. Continue cooking until sauce is creamy and thick. Serve over toast, baked potatoes, pasta or rice.

Serves 4
Each serving equals:
HE: 2 Pr, 1/2 SM, 1/4 Br
149 Calories, 3 gr Fa, 17 gr Pr, 13 gr Ca, 834 mg So
Diabetic: 2 Mt, 1/2 SM, 1/2 St

Cliff called from a truck stop and told me he had just eaten SOS and couldn't I come up with a healthy version. I served this to him when he returned home. He said he liked this way even better.

VEGETABLE PIZZA

1 (8 serving) pkg Crescent refrigerated rolls
1 (8 oz) pkg fat free cream cheese
1/3 cup fat free mayonnaise (8 calories per Tablespoon)
1 Tablespoon reduced calorie dry Ranch Seasoning Mix
3/4 cup chopped cauliflower
3/4 cup chopped broccoli
1/2 cup shredded carrots
1/4 cup diced onion
1/2 cup diced green pepper
3/4 cup sliced fresh mushrooms
1/2 cup sliced radishes
1 1/2 oz shredded reduced fat Cheddar cheese (1/3 cup)

Preheat oven to 450 degrees. Gently pat rolls into 9x13 baking sheet sprayed with olive flavored cooking spray. Bake 5-7 minutes. Cool on wire rack. In small bowl combine cream cheese and mayonnaise. Blend in seasoning mix. Spread over crust. In large bowl combine all fresh vegetables. Sprinkle vegetables evenly over cream cheese. Top with shredded cheddar cheese. Refrigerate until ready to serve.

HINT: 1) If you don't care for any of these fresh veggies, substitute ones you like.

2) DO NOT use inexpensive rolls. They don't cover pan properly.

Serves 8
Each serving equals:
HE: 1 Br, 1 Ve, 3/4 Pr, 5 OC
161 calories, 7 gr Fa, 8 gr Pr, 17 gr Ca, 551 mg So
Diabetic: 1 St, 1 Mt, 1/2 Ve

I love this 'almost salad' on bread.

JOSE'S PARTY PIZZA

1 (8 serving) pkg Crescent Refrigerator rolls
1 (8 oz) pkg fat free cream cheese
1/2 cup chunky salsa
2 teaspoons chili seasoning mix
8 oz ground turkey or beef (90% lean)
1/2 cup frozen corn
10 oz canned red kidney beans, rinsed and drained
2 cups finely shredded lettuce
1 medium tomato, finely diced
1/2 cup chopped green pepper
1/2 cup chopped onion
1/2 cup fat free Catalina Dressing (18 calories per Tbs)
2 1/4 oz finely shredded reduced fat Cheddar or
    Taco cheese (full 1/2 cup)

Preheat oven to 450 degrees. Spray a rimmed 9x13 cookie sheet with olive flavored cooking spray. Pat rolls in pan being sure to seal perforations. Bake 5-7 minutes or until light golden brown. Cool on wire rack. In a medium bowl stir cream cheese with spoon until fluffy. Add salsa and 1 teaspoon chili seasoning mix. Mix well to combine. Spread evenly over cooled crust. In large skillet, sprayed with olive flavored cooking spray, brown meat. Remove from heat. Add corn and kidney beans. Stir. In large bowl combine lettuce, tomato, green pepper and onion. Add cooled meat mixture. Pour Catalina dressing over top. Add remaining 1 teaspoon chili seasoning mix. Mix well to combine. Sprinkle mixture evenly over cream cheese mixture. Sprinkle shredded cheese evenly over top. Chill until ready to serve.

HINT: 1) 16 oz can of kidney beans is 10 oz drained weight.

       2) DO NOT use inexpensive rolls. They don't cover pan properly.

Serves 12
Each serving equals:
HE: 1 1/2 Pr, 3/4 Br, 2/3 Ve, 12 OC
183 calories, 7 gr Fa, 12 gr Pr, 20 gr Ca, 468 mg So
Diabetic: 1 Mt, 1 St, 1 Ve

Add a little spice to the buffet table with this treat.

"DELI SUB" PIZZA

1 (8 serving) pkg Crescent refrigerator rolls
1 (8 oz) pkg fat free cream cheese
1/4 cup fat free mayonnaise (8 calories per Tablespoon)
2 teaspoons yellow mustard
2 cups finely shredded lettuce
4 oz shredded ham (90% lean)
2 1/4 oz shredded reduced fat Cheddar cheese
    (full 1/2 cup)
2 1/4 oz shredded reduced fat Swiss cheese (full 1/2 cup)
2 oz sliced black olives (1/2 cup)
1/2 cup finely diced onion
1 medium tomato, chopped
1/3 cup fat free Italian dressing (4 calories per Tablespoon)

Preheat oven to 450 degrees. Spray a rimmed 9 x 13 cookie sheet with olive flavored cooking spray. Gently pat crescent rolls into pan, being sure to seal perforations. Bake 5-7 minutes. Cool on wire rack. In small bowl combine cream cheese, mayonnaise and yellow mustard. Spread evenly over cooled crust. In large bowl combine shredded lettuce, ham, Cheddar cheese, Swiss cheese, black olives, onion and tomato. Add Italian dressing. Mix gently to coat. Sprinkle lettuce mixture evenly over crust. Chill until ready to serve.

HINT: 1) Carl Buddig Honey Ham works great.

2) DO NOT use inexpensive rolls. They don't cover pan properly.

Serves 8
Each serving equals:
HE: 1 3/4 Pr, 1 Br, 3/4 Ve, 1/4 Fa, 7 OC
236 calories, 12 gr Fa, 13 gr Pr, 19 gr Ca, 1155 mg So
Diabetic: 2 Mt, 1 St, 1 Fa, 1/2 Ve

*I thought of this idea while riding in the car with **Cliff**. He said he's going to have to keep me rollin' along the interstate if I'm thinking of ideas like this!*

DESSERTS

DESSERTS

TOTALLY DECADENT CHOCOLATE CHEESECAKE

1 purchased 9" chocolate crumb pie crust
2 (8 oz) pkgs fat free cream cheese
1/2 cup evaporated skim milk
3/4 cup plain fat free yogurt
2 pkgs Alba chocolate flavored milk drink mix
1 (4 serving) pkg sugar free instant chocolate pudding mix
1 oz chopped almonds (1/4 cup)
1/2 cup reduced calorie whipped topping
    (8 calories per Tablespoon)
4 teaspoons chocolate syrup

In medium bowl whip cream cheese with electric mixer until fluffy. Add skim milk and yogurt, mixing well. Add dry chocolate milk drink mix and dry chocolate pudding mix. Continue beating with electric mixer until blended. Pour into purchased pie crust. Sprinkle chopped almonds on top. Chill at least 2 hours. When serving, top each piece with 1 Tablespoon reduced calorie whipped topping and 1/2 teaspoon chocolate syrup.

Serves 8
Each serving equals:
HE: 1 Pr, 1/2 Br, 1/2 SM, 1/4 Fa, 1 Sl, 6 OC
266 calories, 8 gr Fa, 14 gr Pr, 33 gr Ca, 682 mg So
Diabetic: 1 Mt, 2 St, 1 Fa

If this doesn't take care of your chocolate tooth, I don't know what will.

CHERRY BURRITOS

6 (6 inch) flour tortillas
I (4 serving) pkg sugar free vanilla cook and serve
   pudding mix
3/4 cup water
1 1/2 cups cherries, no sugar added,
   (frozen, fresh or canned)
2-3 drops red food coloring
1/2 teaspoon almond extract
1 teaspoon cinnamon
1 Tablespoon confectioners sugar

Preheat oven to 350 degrees. In medium saucepan combine pudding mix, water and cherries. Cook over medium heat until thick. Add red food coloring and almond extract. Mix well to combine. Remove from heat. Spray a large cookie sheet or jelly roll pan with butter flavored cooking spray. Evenly divide cherry filling and place in center of each tortilla. Fold one edge over filling; roll tightly to opposite side. Place seam side down on cookie sheet. Spray top of each with butter flavored cooking spray. Sprinkle with cinnamon. Bake 10-12 minutes. Quickly respray with butter flavored cooking spray after baking 5 minutes. Remove from oven and dust with confectioners sugar. Good served hot or cold.

Serves 6
Each serving equals:
HE: 1 Br, 1/2 Fr, 18 OC
126 calories, 2 gr Fa, 3 gr Pr, 25 gr Ca, 224 mg So
Diabetic: 1 St, 1/2 Fr

Many a wife has told me these quickly became favorites of their husbands.

CHERRY KOLACHES

12 frozen yeast dinner rolls (80 calories per roll or less)
1 (4 serving) pkg sugar free vanilla cook and serve
    pudding mix
3/4 cup water
2-3 drops red food coloring
1 1/2 cups cherries, no sugar added
    (frozen, fresh or canned)
1/4 teaspoon almond extract

Spray a large cookie sheet with butter flavored cooking spray. Evenly space frozen rolls on sheet. Cover with cloth and let thaw and rise. Make an indentation in center of each roll. In medium saucepan combine pudding mix, water, food coloring and cherries. Cook over medium heat until thick and sauce comes to a boil. Remove from heat. Stir in almond extract. Place 1 large tablespoon of sauce in center of each roll. Cover again and let rolls rest for 10-15 minutes. Quickly spray top of each roll with butter flavored cooking spray. Bake 10-15 minutes at 400 degrees or until golden brown. Remove from oven and quickly spray again with butter flavored cooking spray. Place sheet on top of wire rack and let cool.

Serves 12
Each serving equals:
HE: 1 Br, 1/4 Fr, 7 OC
96 calories, 1 gr Fa, 3 gr Pr, 18 gr Ca, 149 mg So
Diabetic: 1 St

*One of my fondest childhood memories is my mother and grandmother baking kolaches. When I finished experimenting with this recipe, **James** said they were "almost" as good as Grandma's. As these are almost fat and sugar free, I'll accept his compliment.*

PRETZEL "SALAD" DESSERT

4 oz crushed pretzels (2 cups)
Sugar substitute to equal 4 Tablespoons sugar
8 teaspoons reduced calorie margarine
1 (8 oz) pkg fat free cream cheese
2 cups reduced calorie whipped topping
   (8 calories per Tablespoon)
2 cups boiling water
2 (4 serving) pkgs sugar free strawberry gelatin
4 cups strawberries, sliced

In a medium bowl, combine pretzels, 1 Tablespoon sugar substitute and margarine. Press into 9x13 baking dish and bake at 350 degrees for 15 minutes. Cool. Cream together cream cheese, whipped topping and remaining 3 Tablespoons sugar substitute. Spread over crust. Place in freezer at least 1/2 hour but not more than 1 hour. Refrigerate. Mix boiling water and dry gelatin; stir to dissolve. Cool to just lukewarm; add sliced strawberries and pour over all. Chill until firm.

Serves 8
Each serving equals:
HE: 2/3 Br, 1/2 Fr, 1/2 Pr, 1/2 Fa, 1/2 Sl, 3 OC
156 calories, 4 gr Fa, 7 gr Pr, 23 gr Ca, 486 mg So
Diabetic: 1 Fr, 1 Fa, 1/2 Mt, 1/2 St

*My friend **Barb** shares a salad that's really a dessert. But no matter what you call it, the flavor is great.*

RHUBARB TORTE

1 purchased 9" graham cracker pie crust

3/4 cup water

1 (4 serving) pkg sugar free strawberry gelatin

1 (4 serving) pkg sugar free vanilla cook and serve
   pudding mix

4 cups chopped rhubarb

1 (4 serving) pkg sugar free instant vanilla pudding mix

2/3 cup nonfat dry milk powder

1 1/3 cups water

1/2 cup reduced calorie whipped topping
   (8 calories per Tablespoon)

In medium saucepan combine 3/4 cup water, dry gelatin,
cook and serve pudding mix and rhubarb. Cook over
medium heat, stirring constantly until rhubarb is soft and
sauce thickens. Cool slightly. Pour into graham cracker
crust. Chill until set. In medium bowl combine instant
vanilla pudding mix, nonfat dry milk powder and 1 1/3 cups
water. Mix well using a wire whisk. Blend in whipped
topping. Mix well to combine. Spread evenly over top of
rhubarb mixture. Chill until ready to serve.

Serves 8
Each serving equals:
HE: 1 Ve, 1/2 Br, 1/4 SM, 1 Sl, 5 OC
193 calories, 6 gr Fa, 5 gr Pr, 30 gr Ca, 450 mg So
Diabetic: 1 St, 1 Fa, 1 Fr

*A delightful way to enjoy the first rhubarb of the year (or
any time for that matter, if you put some away in the
freezer)*

CARAMEL APPLE DELITE

1 (4 serving) pkg sugar free instant butterscotch
   pudding mix
1 cup + 2 Tablespoons plain fat free yogurt
2 small delicious apples, cored and finely chopped (1 cup)
1 cup crushed pineapple, packed in its own juice,
   undrained
2 oz peanuts, chopped (1/2 cup)
1 oz miniature marshmallows (1/2 cup)
3/4 cup reduced calorie whipped topping
   (8 calories per Tablespoon)

In medium bowl combine pudding mix, yogurt, apples and
pineapple with juice. Add peanuts, marshmallows and
whipped topping. Mix gently to combine. Cover and chill
until ready to serve.

Serves 6 (3/4 cup)
Each serving equals:
HE: 2/3 Fr, 2/3 Fa, 1/3 Pr, 1/4 SM, 1/2 Sl, 9 OC
190 calories, 6 gr Fa, 5 gr Pr, 29 gr Ca, 258 mg So
Diabetic: 1 Fr, 1 Fa, 1 St

A four star winner if ever there was one.

APPLE HARVEST DESSERT

1 (4 serving) pkg sugar free instant vanilla pudding mix
1 cup unsweetened apple juice
1 1/2 cups plain fat free yogurt
1/2 cup reduced calorie whipped topping
  (8 calories per Tablespoon)
1 small apple, chopped (1/2 cup)
1 oz walnuts, chopped (1/4 cup)
1/2 oz miniature marshmallows (1/4 cup)
1 Tablespoon caramel sauce or syrup

In medium bowl combine dry pudding mix and apple juice. Using wire whisk, blend until smooth, about 1 minute. Add yogurt and whipped topping. Stir to combine. Spoon into 6 dessert dishes. Chill at least 2 hours. In small bowl combine chopped apple, walnuts and marshmallows. Divide evenly and sprinkle on top of pudding. Drizzle 1/2 teaspoon caramel sauce on top of each.

Serves 6
Each serving equals:
HE: 1/2 Fr, 1/3 Fa, 1/3 SM, 1/2 Sl, 13 OC
141 calories, 4 gr Fa, 4 gr Pr, 23 gr Ca, 275 mg So
Diabetic: 1 Fr, 1 Fa, 1/2 St

This was created when I was in the middle of an idea and found I didn't have any milk on hand. I think it was meant to be.

BUTTERSCOTCH RICE PUDDING

1 (4 serving) pkg sugar free instant butterscotch
   pudding mix
2 cups skim milk
1/4 cup reduced calorie whipped topping
   (8 calories per Tablespoon)
6 Tablespoons raisins
2 cups cooked rice

In large bowl combine pudding mix and skim milk. Mix well using a wire whisk. Blend in whipped topping. Add raisins and rice. Mix well. Spoon into six dessert dishes. Chill until ready to serve. When serving, good garnished with 1 Tablespoon reduced calorie whipped topping. If using, count optional calories accordingly.

Serves 6
Each serving equals:
HE: 2/3 Br, 1/2 Fr, 1/3 SM, 22 OC
135 calories, less than 1 gr Fa, 4 gr Pr, 29 gr Ca, 265 mg So
Diabetic: 1 St, 1 Fr

I love rice pudding and butterscotch, so it was only natural I find a way to enjoy both flavors at the same time.

ACAPULCO GOLD PUDDING

1 (4 serving) pkg sugar free instant vanilla pudding mix

1/3 cup nonfat dry milk powder

1 cup crushed pineapple, packed in its own juice, undrained

3/4 cup plain fat free yogurt

1 oz sliced almonds (1/4 cup)

2 Tablespoons shredded coconut

Sugar substitute to equal 2 teaspoons sugar

Cinnamon

4 Tablespoons reduced calorie whipped topping
    (8 calories per Tablespoon)

In medium bowl, combine pudding mix and dry milk powder. Add pineapple with juice and yogurt. Mix well using a wire whisk. Add almonds, coconut and sugar substitute. Blend well. Spoon into 4 dessert dishes. Sprinkle dash of cinnamon on top of each. Chill until ready to serve. Just before serving, top each with 1 Tablespoon whipped topping.

Serves 4

Each serving equals:
HE: 1/2 Fr, 1/2 Fa, 1/4 Pr, 1/2 SM, 1/2 Sl,1 OC
170 calories, 5 gr Fa, 6 gr Pr, 26 gr Ca, 394 mg So
Diabetic: 1 Fr, 1 Fa, 1/2 SM

A quick way to impress your family.

DOUG'S DELIGHT

1 (4 serving) pkg sugar free vanilla cook and serve
   pudding mix
2 cups skim milk
1 teaspoon vanilla extract
1 teaspoon cinnamon
1 cup unsweetened applesauce
1/4 cup raisins
1 oz chopped pecans (1/4 cup)
8 slices reduced calorie bread (40 calories per slice),
   broken into large pieces

In large bowl combine dry pudding mix, milk, vanilla and
cinnamon, using a wire whisk. Add applesauce, raisins
and pecans. Add bread pieces. Mix gently to combine.
Cover and chill 1 hour. Pour into 8x8 baking dish sprayed
with butter flavored cooking spray. Bake at 350 degrees
for 45-50 minutes. Serve warm or cold. Good topped with
1 Tablespoon reduced calorie whipped topping. If using
count optional calories accordingly.

Serves 4
Each serving equals:
HE: 1 Fr, 1 Br, 1 Fa, 1/2 SM, 20 OC
252 calories, 5 gr Fa, 11 gr Pr, 41 gr Ca, 386 mg So
Diabetic: 1 Fr, 1 St, 1 Fa, 1/2 SM

Named in honor of our friend **Doug.** *He said it was one of
the best bread puddings he'd eaten and that's his all time
favorite dessert.*

CHEWY FUDGE BROWNIE SUNDAE

4 pkgs Alba chocolate flavored milk drink mix
3 oz quick oats (1 cup)
1 teaspoon baking powder
3 Tablespoons chunky peanut butter, softened to
    room temperature
1 teaspoon vanilla extract
1 cup water
2 cups chocolate or vanilla nonfat ice cream
    (50 calories per 1/2 cup)
4 teaspoons chocolate syrup
4 Tablespoons reduced calorie whipped topping
    (8 calories per Tablespoon)
2 maraschino cherries

Preheat oven to 350 degrees. In large bowl combine dry milk beverage mix, oats and baking powder. Add peanut butter, vanilla and water. Mix to blend. Pour into 8x8 cake pan sprayed with butter flavored cooking spray. Bake 12-15 minutes. Cool on wire rack. Cut into 4 even pieces. When ready to serve, place each brownie on dessert dish. Spread 1/2 cup ice cream over top of each brownie. Drizzle 1 teaspoon chocolate sauce over ice cream. Top with 1 Tablespoon whipped topping. Garnish with 1/2 maraschino cherry.

Serves 4
Each serving equals:
HE: 1 Br, 1 SM, 3/4 Pr, 3/4 Fa, 1/2 Sl, 38 OC
272 calories, 8 gr Fa, 13 gr Pr, 37 gr Ca, 331 mg So
Diabetic: 2 St, 1 Mt, 1 Fa

My sister **Regina** *really enjoyed this when I served it to her.*

APPLESAUCE RAISIN BARS

1 1/2 cups Bisquick reduced fat baking mix
1/2 cups raisins
1 Tablespoon Sprinkle Sweet
1 teaspoon cinnamon
1 1/2 cups unsweetened applesauce
1/2 cup unsweetened apple juice

Preheat oven to 350 degrees. In large bowl combine baking mix, raisins, sugar substitute and cinnamon. Add applesauce and apple juice. Pour into 10 3/4 x 7 x I 1/2 loaf pan. Sprinkle additional cinnamon over top. Bake 25-30 minutes or until a knife inserted comes out clean.

Serves 8 (2 bars each)
Each serving equals:
HE: 1 Fr, 1 Br, 1 OC
146 calories, 2 gr Fa, 2 gr Pr, 30 gr Ca, 251 mg So
Diabetic: 1 Fr, 1 St

A quick way to feed the gang.

TROPICAL FRUIT BARS

1 (8 serving) pkg Crescent refrigerated rolls
1 (8 oz) pkg fat free cream cheese
Sugar substitute to equal 2 Tablespoons sugar
1 cup crushed pineapple, packed in its own juice, drained
1 teaspoon coconut extract
2 medium bananas, sliced
2 cups mandarin oranges, rinsed and drained
6 oz white grapes, sliced (1 cup)
1 (4 serving) pkg sugar free vanilla cook and serve
    pudding mix
1 (4 serving) pkg sugar free lemon gelatin
1 1/2 cups water
2 Tablespoons shredded coconut

Preheat oven to 425 degrees. Spray a 9x13 cookie sheet with rim with butter flavored cooking spray. Pat rolls in pan being sure to seal perforations. Bake 6-8 minutes or until light golden brown. Cool on wire rack. In medium bowl combine cream cheese, sugar substitute, drained crushed pineapple and coconut extract. Spread evenly over cooled crust. Evenly sprinkle sliced bananas, mandarin oranges and sliced grapes over cream cheese mixture. In medium saucepan combine pudding mix, dry gelatin and water. Cook over medium heat until mixture starts to boil, stirring constantly. Drizzle over fruit. Cool 15 minutes. Sprinkle shredded coconut over top. Chill 2 hours before serving. Cut into 16 bars.

HINT: DO NOT use inexpensive rolls. They don't cover pan
       properly.

Serves 16
Each serving equals:
HE: 3/4 Fr, 1/2 Br, 1/4 Pr, 10 OC
103 calories, 3 gr Fa, 4 gr Pr, 15 gr Ca, 251 mg So
Diabetic: 1 Fr, 1/2 St

South Sea Flavor right in your own kitchen.

APPLE APEEL'S

1 (8 serving) pkg Crescent refrigerated rolls
1 (4 serving) pkg sugar free vanilla cook and serve
pudding mix
1 (4 serving) pkg sugar free lemon gelatin
1 1/3 cups water
6 small cooking apples, cored and diced (3 cups)
1 1/2 teaspoons cinnamon
I (8 oz) pkg fat free cream cheese
Sugar substitute to equal 2 Tablespoons sugar

Preheat oven to 425 degrees. Spray a 9x13 cookie sheet
with rim with butter flavored cooking spray. Pat rolls in pan
being sure to seal perforations. Bake 6-8 minutes or until
light golden brown. Cool on wire rack. In medium
saucepan combine pudding mix, dry gelatin and water.
Add apples and 1 teaspoon cinnamon. Cook over medium
heat, stirring constantly, until mixture comes to a boil.
Remove from heat. Cool 15 minutes. Meanwhile, in
medium bowl combine cream cheese, sugar substitute
and 1/2 teaspoon cinnamon. Spread evenly over cooled
crust. Spread cooled apple mixture evenly over top of
cream cheese mixture. Chill about 2 hours. Cut into 16
squares.

HINT: 1. 1/4 cup raisins can be added with apples.

2. DO NOT use inexpensive rolls. They don't
cover the pan properly.

Serves 16
Each serving equals:
HE: 1/2 Br, 1/3 Fr, 1/4 Pr, 8 OC
101 calories, 3 gr Fa, 3 gr Pr, 15 gr Ca, 249 mg So
Diabetic: 1 St, 1/2 Fa

When I served this to the ladies during newsletter week,
Lisa, *who was home from college and helping her mother*
Ruth *with the newsletter, loved them. So I asked her to*
name the bars. I think she did a great job.

APPLE MINCEMEAT PIE

1 purchased 9" unbaked refrigerated pie crust
8 small cooking apples, cored and chopped (4 cups)
3/4 cup raisins
1 cup unsweetened apple juice
1 (4 serving) pkg sugar free lemon gelatin
1 (4 serving) pkg sugar free vanilla cook and serve
   pudding mix
1 Tablespoon Apple Pie Spice
2 teaspoons cider vinegar
1 Tablespoon Brown Sugar Twin

Preheat oven to 375 degrees. In small bowl combine apples and raisins. In large saucepan combine apple juice, dry gelatin, pudding mix, spices, vinegar and brown sugar. Cook over medium heat about 1 minute. Add apple and raisin mixture. Cook about 10 minutes, stirring often. Place pie crust in 8" pie plate. With sharp knife, carefully cut crust off even with edge of plate. Save scraps. Flute edge. Pour apple mixture into crust. Garnish top with pie crust scraps. Bake 45-50 minutes.

Serves 8
Each serving equals:
HE: 2 Fr, 1/2 Br, 1/2 Sl, 25 OC
287 calories, 8 gr Fa, 2 gr Pr, 52 gr Ca, 236 mg So
Diabetic: 2 Fr, 1 St, 1 Fa

HINT: 1 cup canned beef broth can be used in place of
        apple juice, for old time flavor.

*After trying this, **Eva** wrote me and said it was the best mincemeat she had ever eaten.*

SIMPLY SUPERB BANANA CREAM PIE

1 purchased 9" chocolate crumb pie crust
2 medium bananas, sliced
1 (4 serving) pkg sugar free instant banana pudding mix
2/3 cup nonfat dry milk powder
1 1/3 cups water
1 cup reduced calorie whipped topping
    (8 calories per Tablespoon)
1 Tablespoon chocolate syrup

Layer bananas on bottom of pie crust. In medium bowl combine pudding mix and nonfat dry milk powder. Add water. Mix well using a wire whisk. Blend in 1/2 cup whipped topping. Pour over bananas. Chill until set, about 2 hours. Evenly spread remaining 1/2 cup whipped topping over pudding layer. Drizzle chocolate syrup over top. Chill until ready to serve.

Serves 8
Each serving equals:
HE: 1/2 Br, 1/2 Fr, 1/4 SM, 1 Sl, 4 OC
200 calories, 6 gr Fa, 4 gr Pr, 32 gr Ca, 298 mg So
Diabetic: 1 St, 1 Fa, 1 Fr

*When my printer **Tom** insisted this pie was too good to have just any name, I had a pie naming contest. **Dorothy** came up with the winning name. You guessed right if you said **Tom** was the judge.*

BANANA-BUTTERSCOTCH PIE

1 purchased 9" graham cracker pie crust
2 medium bananas
1 (4 serving) pkg sugar free instant butterscotch
   pudding mix
2 cups skim milk
1/2 cup reduced calorie whipped topping
   (8 calories per Tablespoon)

Slice bananas and layer on bottom of pie crust. In medium
mixing bowl combine pudding mix and milk. Mix well using
a wire whisk. Blend in whipped topping. Pour over sliced
bananas. Cover and chill until set, about 2 hours. Good
served with 1 Tablespoon reduced calorie whipped topping
as garnish for each piece. If used, count optional calories
accordingly.

Serves 8
Each serving equals:
HE: 1/2 Br, 1/2 Fr, 1/4 SM, 1/2 Sl, 31 OC
188 calories, 6 gr Fa, 3 gr Pr, 30 gr Ca, 347 mg So
Diabetic: 1 St, 1 Fa, 1 Fr

*I made this for my daughter and son-in-law, **Becky** and
Matt while visiting them. They both said come back
anytime as long as I make another pie.*

BANANA SPLIT PIE

1 purchased 9" chocolate crumb pie crust
1 medium banana
1 cup crushed pineapple, packed in its own juice, drained
1 (4 serving) pkg sugar free instant vanilla pudding mix
2 cups skim milk
1 cup strawberries, sliced
1/2 cup reduced calorie whipped topping
   (8 calories per Tablespoon)
2 teaspoons chocolate syrup
4 maraschino cherries

Slice banana and layer on bottom of chocolate pie crust. Sprinkle pineapple over banana. In medium bowl combine pudding mix and skim milk. Mix well using a wire whisk. Pour over pineapple and banana. Chill about 30 minutes. Slice strawberries on top of pudding. Top with whipped topping. Drizzle chocolate syrup over top. Cut cherries in half and garnish top with cherries. Chill at least 2 hours.

Serves 8
Each serving equals:
HE: 2/3 Fr, 1/2 Br, 1/4 SM, 1 Sl, 1 OC
201 calories, 6 gr Fa, 3 gr Pr, 33 gr Ca, 203 mg So
Diabetic: 1 St, 1 Fr, 1 Fa

HINT: For a firmer pie, you can use 2/3 cup non fat dry milk powder and 1 1/3 cups water in place of 2 cups of skim milk.

Cliff's all time favorite! When I first made it for him, he insisted I make another to take to his co-workers. He said if I ever open a restaurant, people would come for the desserts alone. Do you think he liked it?

FRESH STRAWBERRY PIE

1 prepared 9" pie crust (your choice)
2 cups fresh strawberries, sliced
1 (4 serving) pkg sugar free vanilla cook and serve
   pudding mix
1 (4 serving) pkg sugar free strawberry gelatin
1 1/2 cups water

Place strawberries in pie shell. In medium saucepan combine pudding mix, dry gelatin and water. Cook over medium heat until mixture becomes clear and comes to a boil, stirring constantly. Remove from heat. Pour over sliced strawberries. Chill until set. When serving, good topped with reduced calorie whipped topping. If using, count optional calories accordingly.

Serves 8
Each serving equals:
HE: 1/2 Br, 1/4 Fr, 1/2 Sl, 24 OC
145 calories, 6 gr Fa, 2 gr Pr, 21 gr Ca, 247 mg So
Diabetic: 1 St, 1 Fa, 1/2 Fr

A delightful way to enjoy strawberries.

HAWAIIAN STRAWBERRY PIE

1 purchased 9" graham cracker pie crust

2 cups fresh strawberries, sliced

1 (4 serving) pkg sugar free strawberry gelatin

1 (4 serving) pkg sugar free vanilla cook and serve pudding mix

1 cup crushed pineapple, packed in its own juice, drained (reserve liquid)

1 teaspoon coconut extract

1 cup reduced calorie whipped topping (8 calories per Tablespoon)

2 Tablespoons shredded coconut

Layer strawberries in pie crust. In medium saucepan combine dry gelatin and pudding mix. Add enough water to reserved pineapple juice to make 1 1/2 cups liquid. Add to pudding mixture. Cook over medium heat, stirring constantly, until mixture comes to a boil and becomes clear. Pour hot sauce over strawberries. Chill 2 hours. In small mixing bowl combine drained pineapple, coconut extract and whipped topping. Spread mixture over top of pie. Sprinkle shredded coconut evenly over top. Chill until ready to serve.

Serves 8
Each serving equals:
HE: 1/2 Br, 1/2 Fr, 1 Sl, 4 OC
187 calories, 7 gr Fa, 2 gr Pr, 29 gr Ca, 251 mg So
Diabetic: 1 St, 1 Fa, 1Fr

My all time favorite pie. The combination of pineapple and strawberries is enough to think you're in heaven.

LEMON BLUEBERRY CREAM PIE

1 purchased 9" butter flavored pie crust
1 (4 serving) pkg sugar free lemon gelatin
1 (4 serving) pkg sugar free instant vanilla pudding mix
2/3 cup nonfat dry milk powder
1 1/2 cups water
1 cup reduced calorie whipped topping
  (8 calories per Tablespoon)
1 1/2 cups fresh blueberries

In large bowl combine dry gelatin, dry pudding mix and dry milk powder. Add water; mix well using a wire whisk. Add 1/2 cup reduced calorie whipped topping. Combine well. Gently stir in blueberries. Pour into pie crust. Chill until set, about 2 hours. Spread remaining 1/2 cup whipped topping over top of pie. Chill until ready to serve.

Serves 8
Each serving equals:
HE: 1/2 Br, 1/4 Fr, 1/4 SM, 1 Sl, 3 OC
182 calories, 6 gr Fa, 4 gr Pr, 28 gr Ca, 255 mg So
Diabetic: 1 St, 1 Fa, 1 Fr

*My friend and typist **Shirley** really enjoyed this flavor combination.*

FROZEN LEMON YOGURT PIE

1 purchased 9" butter flavored pie crust
3 cups plain fat free yogurt
1 cup reduced calorie whipped topping
(8 calories per Tablespoon)
2 (4 serving) pkgs sugar free lemon gelatin

In large bowl combine yogurt and whipped topping. Blend in dry gelatin. Mix well. Pour into pie crust. Freeze at least 4 hours. Remove from freezer 30 minutes before serving.

Serves 8
Each serving equals:
HE: 1/2 Br, 1/2 SM, 1/2 Sl, 34 OC
190 calories, 6 gr Fa, 8 gr Pr, 26 gr Ca, 249 mg So
Diabetic: 1 St, 1 Fa, 1/2 SM

HINT: If you like your lemon a little sweeter, add sugar
substitute to equal 2 teaspoons sugar when
blending in gelatin.

*I created this while visiting with **Barb** in the swimming pool at our local health center. I had to rush home to try the idea out before going to work. Am I ever glad I did.*

CHERRY BANANA PIE

1 purchased 9" butter flavored pie crust
1 (4 serving) pkg sugar free vanilla cook and serve
   pudding mix
1 (4 serving) pkg sugar free cherry gelatin
1 1/3 cups water
2 cups canned cherries, packed in water, drained
1 teaspoon almond extract
2 medium bananas
3/4 cup plain fat free yogurt
1/3 cup non fat dry milk powder
2 Tablespoons Sprinkle Sweet
1 cup reduced calorie whipped topping
   (8 calories per Tablespoon)
1/2 oz finely chopped almonds (2 Tablespoons)

In a medium saucepan combine pudding mix, dry gelatin, water and cherries. Cook over medium heat until mixture comes to a boil, stirring constantly. Remove from heat, stir in 1/2 teaspoon almond extract. Cool 10 minutes. Slice bananas into cherry mixture. Stir gently to combine. Pour into pie crust. Chill at least 2 hours. In medium bowl combine yogurt, dry milk powder and sugar substitute. Blend in whipped topping. Spread evenly over filling. Sprinkle chopped almonds over top. Chill until ready to serve.

Serves 8
Each serving equals:
HE: 1 Fr, 1/2 Br, 1/4 SM, 1 Sl, 9 OC
231 calories, 7 gr Fa, 5 gr Pr, 37 gr Ca, 261 mg So
Diabetic: 1 Fr, 1 St, 1 Fa

I love old recipes. I found the basis for this in an OPEN LINE bulletin that was 20 years old. I took the most of the fats and sugar out and left the flavor in. Thanks **DWAYNE.**

NEW "OLD FASHIONED" CHERRY CHEESECAKE

1 purchased 9" graham cracker pie crust
2 (8 oz) pkgs fat free cream cheese
2/3 cup nonfat dry milk powder
Sugar substitute to equal 2 Tablespoons sugar
1 teaspoon vanilla extract
1 cup reduced calorie whipped topping
(8 calories per Tablespoon)
1 (4 serving) pkg sugar free cherry gelatin
1 (4 serving) pkg sugar free vanilla cook and serve
pudding mix
2 cups canned cherries, packed in water, drained
(reserve liquid)

In large bowl stir cream cheese with spoon until soft. Add dry milk powder, sugar substitute and vanilla extract. Blend in 1/2 cup reduced calorie whipped topping. Spread evenly over bottom of pie crust. Chill. In medium saucepan combine dry cherry gelatin and pudding mix. Add enough water to reserved cherry liquid to make 3/4 cup. Add to saucepan. Mix well. Add cherries. Cook over medium heat until mixture comes to a boil, stirring constantly, being sure not to crush cherries. Cool completely. Spoon over cream cheese mixture. Chill at least 2 hours. When serving, garnish each piece with 1 Tablespoon reduced calorie whipped topping.

Serves 8
Each serving equals:
HE: 1 Pr, 1/2 Br, 1/2 Fr, 1/4 SM, 1 Sl, 2 OC
244 calories, 7 gr Fa, 12 gr Pr, 33 gr Ca, 623 mg So
Diabetic: 1 Mt, 1 St, 1 Fr, 1/2 Fa

A taste treat to be remembered for days.

PEACH MELBA PIE

1 purchased 9" butter flavored pie crust
4 medium peaches, peeled and sliced
1 (4 serving) pkg sugar free vanilla cook and serve
    pudding mix
1 (4 serving) pkg sugar free raspberry gelatin
1 1/3 cups water
3 cups fresh or frozen raspberries,
    slightly thawed, no sugar added
1/2 cup reduced calorie whipped topping
    (8 calories per Tablespoon)

Layer sliced peaches in bottom of pie crust. In medium saucepan combine pudding mix, dry gelatin and water. Cook over medium heat until mixture starts to boil, stirring constantly. Remove from heat. Gently stir in raspberries. Pour hot mixture over peaches. Chill at least 2 hours. When serving, top each piece with 1 Tablespoon reduced calorie whipped topping.

Serves 8
Each serving equals:
HE: 1 Fr, 1/2 Br, 1/2 Sl, 32 OC
186 calories, 6 gr Fa, 3 gr Pr, 30 gr Ca, 222 mg So
Diabetic: 1 Fr, 1 St, 1 Fa

What a way to enjoy the flavor of peaches and raspberries!

CRUSTLESS PUMPKIN PIE

1/2 cup Bisquick Reduced Fat baking mix
1 (4 serving) pkg sugar free instant vanilla pudding mix
2 cups canned pumpkin
1 1/2 cups evaporated skim milk
2 eggs or equivalent in egg substitute
2 Tablespoons Brown Sugar Twin
2 teaspoons pumpkin pie spice

Preheat oven to 350 degrees. Spray a 9" pie pan with cooking spray. In large bowl combine baking mix and dry pudding mix. Add pumpkin, milk, eggs, Brown Sugar Twin and pumpkin pie spice. Using an electric mixer, blend for 2 minutes. Pour into sprayed pie pan. Bake 50 minutes or until center is puffed up.

Serves 8
Each serving equals:
HE: 1/2 Ve, 1/3 SM, 1/3 Br, 1/4 Pr (limited) 21 OC
117 calories, 2 gr Fa, 7 gr Pr, 19 gr Ca, 318 mg So
Diabetic: 1 St, 1/2 SM

Hold the crust, but not the flavor!

PUMPKIN HOLIDAY PIE

1 purchased 9" graham cracker pie crust
1 (8 oz) pkg fat free cream cheese
1/3 cup nonfat dry milk powder
Sugar substitute to equal 2 Tablespoons sugar
1 teaspoon vanilla extract
1 cup reduced calorie whipped topping
   (8 calories per Tablespoon)
1 1/2 cups evaporated skim milk
2 cups canned pumpkin
2 teaspoons pumpkin pie spice
2 (4 serving) pkgs sugar free instant vanilla pudding mix

In large bowl stir cream cheese with spoon until soft. Add dry milk powder, sugar substitute and vanilla extract. Blend in 1/2 cup whipped topping. Spread evenly over bottom of crust. In medium bowl combine evaporated skim milk, canned pumpkin and pumpkin pie spice. Add dry pudding mix. Mix well using a wire whisk. Pour over cream cheese mixture. Chill until set, about 2 hours. When serving, top each piece with 1 Tablespoon reduced calorie whipped topping.

Serves 8
Each serving equals:
HE: 1/2 Br, 1/2 Pr, 1/2 SM, 1/2 Ve, 1 Sl, 13 OC
256 calories, 7 gr Fa, 11 gr Pr, 37 gr Ca, 714 mg So
Diabetic: 1 1/2 St, 1 SM, 1 Fa

A pie that's a treat to both the eyes and tummy.

RAISIN "SOUR CREAM" PIE

1 purchased 9" unbaked refrigerated pie crust,
   baked and cooled
1 (4 serving) pkg sugar free vanilla cook and serve
   pudding mix
1 cup skim milk
1/2 cup water
1 cup raisins
1/2 teaspoon vanilla extract
1 1/4 cups plain fat free yogurt
Sugar substitute to equal 2 Tablespoons sugar
1 cup reduced calorie whipped topping
   (8 calories per Tablespoon)
1/2 teaspoon nutmeg

In medium saucepan, combine pudding mix, milk, water
and raisins. Cook over medium heat until pudding comes
to a boil, stirring constantly. Remove from heat. Stir in
vanilla. Cool in pan for about 15 minutes. Add yogurt and
sugar substitute. Pour into cooled baked pie crust. Chill at
least 3 hours. Combine whipped topping and nutmeg.
Spread over chilled pie. Continue chilling until ready to
serve.

Serves 8
Each serving equals:
HE: 1 Fr, 1/2 Br, 1/3 SM, 1/2 Sl, 37 OC
210 calories, 8 gr Fa, 5 gr Pr, 29 gr Ca, 252 mg So
Diabetic: 1 Fr, 1 St, 1 Fa, 1/2 SM

*When **Michael,** my friend **Gayle's** husband said this was a
keeper, it was no light compliment. He's a true sour cream
pie lover.*

"CANDY BAR" PIE

1 purchased 9" chocolate crumb pie crust
2 oz peanuts, coarsely chopped (1/2 cup)
3 Tablespoons caramel syrup
1 (4 serving) pkg sugar free instant chocolate pudding mix
2/3 cup nonfat dry milk powder
1 1/2 cups water
1/2 cup reduced calorie whipped topping
   (8 calories per Tablespoon)

Place 1/3 cup peanuts evenly over bottom of pie crust. Drizzle 2 Tablespoons caramel syrup over peanuts. Combine pudding mix, dry milk powder and water using a wire whisk. Pour over peanuts. Chill at least 2 hours. Spread whipped topping evenly over chilled pie. Sprinkle remaining peanuts over whipped topping. Drizzle remaining 1 Tablespoon caramel syrup over top.

Serves 8
Each serving equals:
HE: 1/2 Br, 1/2 Fa, 1/4 SM, 1/4 Pr, 1 Sl, 7 OC
229 calories, 9 gr Fa, 5 gr Pr, 32 gr Ca, 318 mg So
Diabetic: 2 St, 1 Fa

*This was created when **STEPHANIE** told me her daughter loved Snicker candy bars, and could I come up with something to take their place.*

TRIPLE LAYER PARTY PIE

1 purchased 9" chocolate crumb pie crust
1 (4 serving) pkg sugar free instant butterscotch
    pudding mix
1 1/3 cups nonfat dry milk powder
2 1/2 cups water
1 (4 serving) pkg sugar free instant chocolate pudding mix
1/2 cup reduced calorie whipped topping
    (8 calories per Tablespoon)
1/2 oz chopped pecans (2 Tablespoons)
1/4 oz mini chocolate chips (1 Tablespoon)

In medium bowl combine butterscotch pudding mix, 2/3 cup nonfat dry milk powder and 1 1/4 cups water. Mix well using a wire whisk. Pour into chocolate crumb pie crust. In medium bowl combine chocolate pudding mix, remaining 2/3 cup nonfat dry milk powder and remaining 1 1/4 cups water. Mix well using a wire whisk. Pour over butterscotch layer. Chill until set. Before serving evenly spread 1/2 cup reduced calorie whipped topping over chocolate layer. Sprinkle pecans and mini chocolate chips evenly over top. Chill until ready to serve.

Serves 8
Each serving equals:
HE: 1/2 Br, 1/2 SM, 1/4 Fa, 1 Sl, 8 OC
217 calories, 7 gr Fa, 6 gr Pr, 32 gr Ca, 487 mg So
Diabetic: 2 St, 1 Fa, 1/2 SM

You can have a party in your mouth with the flavors of this pie. At least that's what **Vince** *said.*

THIS N THAT

THIS AND THAT

RHUBARB SAUCE

4 cups chopped rhubarb
1/4 cup water
1 (4 serving) pkg sugar free strawberry gelatin

In large saucepan combine rhubarb and water. Cook over medium heat, stirring often until rhubarb becomes soft. Add dry strawberry gelatin mixing well to combine. Remove from heat. Chill until ready to serve.

Serves 4 (3/4 cup)
Each serving equals:
HE: 2 Ve, 8 OC
34 calories, 0 gr Fa, 2 gr Pr, 6 gr Ca, 59 mg So
Diabetic: 1/2 Fr

Prepare rhubarb sauce this way and you won't even miss the sugar.

FRESH FRUIT REFRIGERATOR JAM

3 cups fresh fruit of your choice
 (apricots, strawberries, blackberries or raspberries)
1 (4 serving) pkg sugar free lemon gelatin
1 pouch liquid Certo
2 Tablespoons Sprinkle Sweet

Coarsely chop fruit, if necessary. Place fruit in medium saucepan. Mash slightly with potato masher. Add dry lemon gelatin. Cook over medium heat until mixture comes to a full boil, about 5 minutes. Add liquid Certo and Sprinkle Sweet. Continue boiling about 1 minute. Pour into containers. Let cool 30 minutes. Cover and refrigerate overnight before using. Will keep up to 3 weeks in refrigerator.

Makes about 2 cups (1 Tablespoon serving)
Each serving equals:
HE: 11 OC
11 calories, 0 gr Fa, 0 gr Pr, 3 gr Ca, 10 mg So
Diabetic: 1 Free Food

*I love thick jam. So, when my friend **Barb** brought me fresh blackberries from the timber, I tried out Blackberry Jam. When that turned out, I rode my bike to the store for more fruit and tried apricot and strawberry as well. The sugar free lemon gelatin helps to sweeten as well as give that tartness fresh lemon juice would.*

BREAKFAST BREAD PUDDING

4 slices reduced calorie bread, toasted
  (40 calories per slice)
2 Tablespoons peanut butter (chunky or creamy)
2 Tablespoons spreadable fruit (any flavor)
1 (4 serving) pkg sugar free instant vanilla pudding mix
2 cups skim milk

Spread each slice of toast with peanut butter and spreadable fruit. Cut into small cubes. Place evenly in four dessert dishes. In medium bowl combine pudding mix and skim milk. Mix well using a wire whisk. Pour 1/2 cup pudding over toast cubes in each dish. Chill several hours before serving.

Serves 4
Each serving equals:
HE: 1/2 Pr, 1/2 Br, 1/2 Fa, 1/2 Fr, 1/2 SM, 25 OC
180 calories, 4 gr Fa, 9 gr Pr, 27 gr Ca, 519 mg So
Diabetic: 2 St, 1 Mt

Make this easy pudding before you go to bed and enjoy it the next morning for breakfast.

CINNAMON-APPLE CORN BREAD

1 cup yellow cornmeal
1/2 cup flour
1/4 cup Sprinkle Sweet
2 teaspoons baking powder
1/4 teaspoon salt
1/2 teaspoon cinnamon
1 egg or equivalent in egg substitute
1 cup unsweetened applesauce
2 Tablespoons + 2 teaspoons cooking oil

Preheat oven to 350 degrees. In large bowl combine cornmeal, flour, Sprinkle Sweet, baking powder, salt and cinnamon. In small bowl blend egg, applesauce and oil together. Add to dry ingredients. Blend until just moistened. Pour into an 8x8 baking dish sprayed with butter flavored cooking spray. Bake 20-25 minutes.

Serves 8
Each serving equals:
HE: 1 1/3 Br, 3/4 Fa, 1/4 Fr, 10 OC
140 calories, 4 gr Fa, 3 gr Pr, 22 gr Ca, 155 mg So
Diabetic: 1 St, 1 Fa, 1/2 Fr

*My sister **Mary** commented she had been searching for the flavor of this cornbread after enjoying it while on vacation. Well here it is, and you don't even need to leave home.*

PANCAKES WITH APPLESAUCE RAISIN TOPPING

1 cup unsweetened applesauce
1/4 cup raisins
1/2 teaspoon cinnamon
Sugar substitute to equal 1 Tablespoon sugar
3/4 cup Bisquick reduced fat baking mix
1/3 cup nonfat dry milk powder
1 egg or equivalent in egg substitute
1/3 cup water

In small saucepan combine applesauce, raisins, cinnamon and sugar substitute. Simmer over low heat until pancakes are done. In medium bowl combine Bisquick and dry skim milk powder. Add egg and water. Mix with wire whisk until well blended. Spray hot skillet or griddle with butter flavored cooking spray. Pour scant 1/4 cup batter for 4 pancakes. Cook until golden brown. Top each pancake with 1/4 cup hot applesauce mixture.

Serves 4
Each serving equals:
HE: 1 Fr, 1 Br, 1/4 SM, 1/4 Pr (limited) 2 OC
187 calories, 3 gr Fa, 6 gr Pr, 34 gr Ca, 298 mg So
Diabetic: 1 Fr, 1 St

The applesauce "syrup" works great with the pancakes. It's good anytime, but on a brisk fall morning, as my kids use to say,"It's yummy in the tummy!"

SAGE STUFFING BAKE

1/2 cup chopped celery
1/2 cup chopped onion
1 teaspoon dried crushed sage
1/8 teaspoon pepper
6 oz unseasoned whole wheat and white dry
    bread cubes (4 cups)
2 cups Campbells Healthy Request chicken broth

Preheat oven to 350 degrees. In large saucepan, sprayed with butter flavored cooking spray, saute celery and onion over medium heat. Cook and stir until tender. Add sage, pepper and bread cubes. Stir to blend. Gradually pour chicken broth over bread mixture. Toss gently to evenly moisten. Place stuffing mixture in an 8x8 baking dish sprayed with butter flavored cooking spray. Cover. Bake 40-45 minutes.

Serves 8
Each serving equals:
HE: 1 Br, 1/4 Ve, 4 OC
92 calories, less than 1 gr Fa, 3 gr Pr, 18 gr Ca, 446 mg So
Diabetic: 1 St

Who says we can't enjoy stuffing without guilt. This virtually fat free version has all the flavor of traditional stuffing.

APPLE MUFFINS

1 1/2 cups flour
1 teaspoon baking powder
1/2 teaspoon baking soda
1/2 teaspoon salt
1 1/2 teaspoons apple pie spice
3 Tablespoons Sprinkle Sweet
2 small apples, peeled, cored and finely diced (1 cup)
2 Tablespoons oil
1 egg, slightly beaten or equivalent in egg substitute
3/4 cup lowfat buttermilk

Preheat oven to 400 degrees. Spray an 8 hole muffin tin with cooking spray. In large bowl combine flour, baking powder, baking soda, salt, apple pie spice and Sprinkle Sweet. Add apples and mix to blend. In small bowl combine oil, egg and buttermilk. Add to flour mixture. Mix lightly, just to combine. Fill muffin cups. Bake 20 minutes or until golden brown.

Serves 8
Each serving equals:
HE: 1 Br, 3/4 Fa, 1/4 Fr, 20 OC
157 calories, 5 gr Fa, 4 gr Pr, 25 gr Ca, 254 mg So
Diabetic: 1 St, 1 Fa, 1/2 Fr

*When **Mary Anne**, a subscriber from Illinois, wanted a muffin recipe, I created this. I had just purchased crisp juicy apples at a road stand so they were a natural inclusion in the recipe. My husband, **Cliff** really went for these when I made them.*

APRICOT CRESCENT COFFEECAKE

1 (4 serving) pkg sugar free vanilla cook and serve
   pudding mix
1 cup water
18 dried apricot halves, chopped (1 cup)
1/4 cup raisins
1 (8 serving) pkg Crescent refrigerated rolls

Preheat oven to 400 degrees. In medium saucepan combine pudding mix, water, apricots and raisins. Cook over medium heat, stirring constantly, until mixture comes to a boil. Remove from heat. Cool 15-20 minutes. Place rolls on large cookie sheet. Pat into a 14x9 rectangle, being sure to seal perforations. Evenly spread apricot filling over rolls. Roll up like a jelly roll starting with long side. Seal edge well. Place sealed edge down. Curve into a large crescent shape. Gently make several slashes in top. Bake 15-20 minutes. Quickly spray top with butter flavored cooking spray.

Serves 8
Each serving equals:
HE: 1 Br, 2/3 Fr, 10 OC
142 calories, 6 gr Fa, 2 gr Pr, 20 gr Ca, 301 mg So
Diabetic: 1/2 St, 1 Fr, 1 Fa

My Bohemian heritage comes out when I yearn for the types of foods my mother and grandmother would bake. This coffeecake is an example. It is so simple, yet tastes like you spent hours slaving over an oven. Try it on your family one of these weekends and see if it doesn't become a family favorite.

APRICOT-RAISIN NUT BREAD

1 1/2 cups flour
1 teaspoon baking powder
1 teaspoon baking soda
1 teaspoon cinnamon
12 dried apricot halves, chopped (2/3 cup)
1/4 cup raisins
1 oz chopped walnuts (1/4 cup)
1 cup unsweetened apple juice
1/4 cup Sprinkle Sweet
2 eggs or equivalent in egg substitute
2 Tablespoons vegetable oil
1 teaspoon vanilla extract

Preheat oven to 350 degrees. Lightly spray a 4x8 loaf pan with cooking spray. In a large bowl combine flour, baking powder, baking soda and cinnamon. Mix well. Add apricots, raisins and walnuts. In a medium bowl combine apple juice, Sprinkle Sweet, eggs, vegetable oil and vanilla extract. Beat with a wire whisk until well blended. Add liquid mixture to dry mixture. Mix well until combined. Pour into loaf pan. Bake 30-35 minutes or until toothpick inserted in center of loaf comes out clean. Set pan on wire rack and cool.

Serves 12
Each serving equals:
HE: 2/3 Br, 2/3 Fa, 1/2 Fr, 1/4 Pr, 2 OC
133 calories, 5 gr Fa, 3 gr Pr, 19 gr Ca, 106 mg So
Diabetic: 1 Fr, 1 Fa, 1/2 St

__Lydia__, a member of the Illinois Cancer Awareness Group asked me to create a bread high in Beta Carotene. My husband, __Cliff__ took a loaf of this bread with him in the truck and he said it stayed moist all week. He wanted me to make another loaf as soon as he got home.

PUMPKIN-RAISIN BREAD

1 cup plus 2 Tablespoons flour
1/3 cup sugar
1 teaspoon baking soda
1/2 teaspoon baking powder
1 cup canned pumpkin
2 eggs or equivalent in egg substitute
1/4 cup vegetable oil
1 teaspoon vanilla extract
3/4 cup raisins
1 oz chopped walnuts (1/4 cup)

Preheat oven to 375 degrees. Lightly spray an 8 1/2 x 4 1/2 x 2 1/2 loaf pan with non-stick cooking spray. In medium mixing bowl combine flour, sugar, baking soda and baking powder. In large mixing bowl combine pumpkin, eggs, oil and vanilla extract. Mix well to blend. Add flour mixture to pumpkin mixture. Stir until moistened. Add raisins and walnuts. Stir until combined. Pour batter into pan. Bake 45-50 minutes or until toothpick inserted in center comes out dry. Set pan on wire rack and cool.

Serves 12
Each serving equals:
HE: 1 Fa, 1/2 Br, 1/2 Fr, 1/4 Pr, 33 OC
175 calories, 7 gr Fa, 3 gr Pr, 25 gr Ca, 94 mg So
Diabetic: 1 Fa, 1 St, 1 Fr

*Here's another bread I created for **Lydia** and the Illinois Cancer Awareness Group. It's wonderful any time of the year, but especially during the fall months.*

VEGGIE SALAD SANDWICH FILLING

1/2 cup chopped green pepper
1/2 cup chopped cucumber, seeded and peeled
1 medium tomato, finely chopped
1/2 cup finely chopped celery
1/4 cup chopped onion
2 Tablespoons snipped parsley
2 Tablespoons dill pickle relish
1/8 teaspoon lemon pepper
1 (8 oz) pkg fat free cream cheese
1/4 cup fat free mayonnaise (8 calories per Tablespoon)

In large bowl combine green pepper, cucumber, tomato, celery, onion, parsley and dill pickle relish. Add lemon pepper, cream cheese and mayonnaise. Gently mix to combine. Cover and chill until ready to serve. Good on reduced calorie Italian Bread (40 calories per slice). Also good with 1 slice reduced calorie cheese on bread. If using, count additional exchange accordingly.

Serves 4   (3/4 cup)
Each serving equals:
HE: 1 1/4 Ve, 1 Pr, 8 OC
77 calories, 0 gr Fa, 9 gr Pr, 9 gr Ca, 511 mg So
Diabetic: 1 Ve, 1 Mt

Don't turn your nose up at this one until you try it. The flavors of the veggies blend wonderful with the fat free cream cheese. I loved it both with and without the added slice of reduced fat American Cheese.

PARTY MIX

1/2 cup reduced calorie margarine
1/2 cup fat free Italian Dressing
  (4 calories per Tablespoon)
2 Tablespoons Worcestershire sauce
1/2 teaspoon garlic salt
4 1/2 oz Rice Chex (5 cups)
7 1/2 oz Wheat Chex (5 cups)
4 oz Cheerios (5 cups)
5 oz pretzels, coarsely broken (2 1/2 cups)

Preheat oven to 250 degrees. In medium saucepan combine margarine, Italian Dressing, Worcestershire sauce and garlic salt. Cook over medium heat, stirring constantly 3 minutes. In very large bowl combine Rice Chex, Wheat Chex, Cheerios and pretzels. Drizzle slightly cooled margarine mixture over top. Mix well. Spray 2 large cookie sheets or jelly roll pans with butter flavored cooking spray. Evenly spread mixture in pans. Bake 60 minutes, stirring every 15 minutes. Store in airtight container.

Serves 16   (1 full cup)
Each serving equals:
HE: 1 3/4 Br, 3/4 Fa, 2 OC
162 calories, 3 gr Fa, 3 gr Pr, 31 gr Ca, 533 mg So
Diabetic: 2 St

Cliff is a true snack lover and the traditional party mix is his all time favorite snack. So, when he asked me if I couldn't come up with SOMETHING low fat along those lines, I put my thinking cap on and created this just for him. But he doesn't mind sharing with you.

CHOCOLATE-PECAN CLUSTERS

1/2 oz miniature marshmallows (1/4 cup)
1/2 oz mini chocolate chips (1 Tablespoon)
1 teaspoon reduced calorie margarine
1/4 teaspoon vanilla extract
7/8 oz chopped pecans (3 Tablespoons + 1 1/2 teaspoons)

Place marshmallows, chocolate chips and margarine in 2 cup glass measure. Cover and microwave on high 30 seconds. Add vanilla and stir until smooth. Add pecans. Mix to coat completely. Drop by small teaspoons to form 8 clusters on wax paper. Chill until firm, about 30 minutes.

HINT: Don't double recipe. It works best in the amounts given.

Serves 4 (2 each)
Each serving equals:
HE: 1 Fa, 31 OC
82 calories, 6 gr Fa, 1 gr Pr, 6 gr Ca, 6 mg So
Diabetic: 1 Fa, 1/2 St

I had so many requests for a Christmas Candy, it would make Santa's head spin. I think you will be pleased with this. But, remember it's important you practice portion control, or I won't give you another candy recipe, ever! (No you don't need to prepare and sample these four times before company comes, to be sure you have them down just right.)

CHOCOLATE RUM BALLS

2/3 cup nonfat dry milk powder
1 (4 serving) pkg sugar free instant chocolate pudding mix
6 (2 1/2") graham cracker squares
1 teaspoon vanilla extract
1/2 teaspoon rum extract
6 Tablespoons water

In medium bowl combine dry milk powder and pudding mix. Crush graham crackers and add crumbs to milk mixture. Mix well. In small bowl combine vanilla extract, rum extract and water. Add to dry mixture. Mix gently to combine. Roll into 12 balls. Cover and chill.

HINT: 1) A sandwich bag works great for making graham cracker crumbs.

2) If mixture is too dry, add a few drops of water at a time.

Serves 6 (2 balls each)
Each serving equals:
HE: 1/3 SM, 1/3 Br, 17 OC
84 calories, 1 gr Fa, 4 gr Pr, 15 gr Ca, 299 mg So
Diabetic: 1 St

These tasty treats are very quick to put together. But, it's up to you whether you let on they are.

HAM-SPINACH DIP

1 (8 oz) pkg fat free cream cheese
3/4 cup plain fat free yogurt
1/3 cup nonfat dry milk powder
1/2 cup fat free mayonnaise
   (8 calories per Tablespoon)
1 teaspoon Italian Seasoning
4 oz finely diced ham, (90% lean)
1 (10 oz) pkg frozen chopped spinach,
   thawed and thoroughly drained

In medium bowl stir cream cheese with spoon until fluffy. Add yogurt, nonfat dry milk powder, mayonnaise and Italian Seasoning. Continue mixing until well blended. Add diced ham and drained spinach. Mix gently to combine. Cover and chill until ready to serve.

HINT: 1) Dubuque 97% fat free ham works great.

       2) It's wonderful on a baked potato.

Serves 6 (1/2 cup)
Each serving equals:
HE: 1 1/3 Pr, 1/2 Ve, 1/3 SM, 11 OC
109 calories, 1 gr Fa, 13 gr Pr, 12 gr Ca, 634 mg So
Diabetic: 1 1/2 Mt, 2 Ve

***Cliff** hates spinach. But, he enjoyed this dip. Now, if I could only think of some way to include broccoli, I'd have it made.*

RIO GRANDE DIP

1 1/2 cups plain fat free yogurt
3 oz finely shredded reduced fat Cheddar cheese (3/4 cup)
1/4 cup fat free mayonnaise (8 calories per Tablespoon)
2 Tablespoons Taco seasoning mix
2 Tablespoons finely diced onion
2 Tablespoons finely diced green pepper

In medium bowl combine yogurt, cheese and mayonnaise. Add Taco seasoning, onion and green pepper. Mix well. Cover and chill until ready to use. Makes 2 cups.

Serves 8 (1/4 cup each)
Each serving equals:
HE: 1/2 Pr, 1/4 SM, 4 OC
61 calories, 2 gr Fa, 6 gr Pr, 5 gr Ca, 180 mg So
Diabetic: 1/2 SM

*If you really like the feeling of smoke coming out your ears, the way **Cliff** does, just add more Taco seasoning mix to the recipe. But, for most of us "wimps", 2 Tablespoons is just enough.*

MOCHA

1 (8 oz) cup hot coffee
1 pkg sugar free hot chocolate beverage drink
1 Tablespoon reduced calorie whipped topping
   (8 calories per Tablespoon)

In large mug mix beverage drink into hot coffee. Stir well to blend. Top with 1 Tablespoon reduced calorie whipped topping and enjoy.

Serves 1
Each serving equals:
HE: 1 SM, 8 OC
80 calories, 1 gr Fa, 6 gr Pr, 12 gr Ca, 172 mg So
Diabetic: 1 SM

*My daughter **Becky** sent me her favorite way to fix a quick hot chocolate.*

MULLED CRANBERRY DRINK

6 cups low calorie cranberry juice cocktail
2 cups Dole Pure and Light mandarin-tangerine juice
2 teaspoons pumpkin pie spice

In a large saucepan combine cranberry juice, mandarin-tangerine juice and pumpkin pie spice. Slowly bring mixture to a boil. Reduce heat. Simmer 20 minutes.

Serves 8 (1 cup)
Each serving equals:
HE: 1 1/2 Fr
62 calories, 0 gr Fa, 0 gr Pr, 15 gr Ca, 6 mg So
Diabetic: 1 Fr

This just might be the beverage you have been looking for to serve at your next party.

COOKING TIPS

COOKING TIPS

A very good white sauce for vegetables and casseroles without using added fat can be made by spraying a saucepan with butter flavored cooking spray. Place 1 1/2 cups evaporated skim milk and 3 Tablespoons flour in a covered jar. Mix well. Pour into sprayed saucepan and cook over medium heat until thick, stirring constantly. Add salt and pepper to taste. You can also add 1/2 cup canned drained mushrooms and/or 3 oz. shredded reduced fat cheese (3/4 cup). Continue cooking until cheese melts.

If you place 1 cup of plain fat free yogurt in a sieve lined with a coffee filter, and place the sieve over a small bowl and refrigerate for about 6 hours, you will end up with a very good alternative for sour cream.

For a special treat that tastes anything but "diet", try placing spreadable fruit in a container and microwave for about 15 seconds. Then pour melted fruit over a serving of nonfat ice cream or frozen yogurt. 1 tablespoon of spreadable fruit is equal to 1 fruit serving. Some combinations to get you started are apricot over chocolate ice cream; strawberry over strawberry ice cream, or any flavor over vanilla.

The next time you are making treats for the family, try using unsweetened applesauce for some or all of the required oil in the recipe. For instance, if the recipe calls for 1/2 cup cooking oil, use up to the 1/2 cup in applesauce. It works and most people will not even notice the difference. It's great in purchased cake mixes, but so far I haven't been able to figure out a way to deep fat fry with it!

Heat 2 cups drained canned or frozen green beans. Add 1/2 cup chunky salsa and heat through. Chunky salsa also makes a wonderful dressing on lettuce salads. It only counts as a vegetable, so enjoy.

For a different taste when preparing sugar free instant pudding mixes, use 3/4 cup plain fat free yogurt for one of the required cups of milk. Blend as usual. It will be thicker and creamier. And, no it doesn't taste like yogurt.

The next time you warm canned vegetables, such as carrots or green beans, drain and heat the vegetables in 1/4 cup beef or chicken broth. It gives a nice variation to an old standby.

I'm going to let you in on my secret for making "Grandma's Lemonade". Use purchased sugar free lemonade mix. Prepare it according to the package directions. Then, slice 1/3 to 1/2 of a lemon, (rind, seeds and all). Pour about 2 cups of the prepared lemonade into a blender. Add the lemon chunks and blend on high for 20-30 seconds or until the lemon almost disappears. Pour back into the pitcher of prepared lemonade and stir well. Serve over ice and enjoy. It tastes just like Grandma used to make...and, I won't tell our secret, if you don't.

If you are preparing a pie filling that has ample moisture to it, just line graham crackers in the bottom of an 9x9 cake pan. Pour the filling over the top of the crackers. Cover and chill until the moisture has enough time to work down to the crackers and make them soft. Overnight is best. This eliminates the added fats and sugars of a pie crust.

Low fat cooking sprays are one of the new wonders of the modern world. So far, it comes in three flavors. I use OLIVE when cooking Mexican or Italian, BUTTER when the hint of butter is desired and REGULAR for everything else. You can quickly spray air-popped popcorn with butter flavored for a low fat taste treat. It's also good on fresh cooked corn on the cob. Now, if the manufacturers would come out with bacon and caramel flavors in **air pump** containers, we'd have it made!

Don't give nonfat dry milk powder a "bum steer". It's great! I DO NOT use it for drinking, but I DO use it for cooking. Three reasons why are: (1) It is very inexpensive, (2) It does not sour because you use it only as needed. (3) When used in puddings, 2/3 cup powder plus 1 1/2 cups water equals 2 cups of skim milk in nutrients, but you don't have all the liquid, so your pudding is much thicker and sets up within minutes. Nonfat Dry Milk Powder, Mother Nature's modern day convenience.

The next time you want to enjoy a "fruit shake" with some pizazz, just combine soda water and unsweetened fruit juice in a blender. Add crushed ice. Blend on high until thick. Refreshment without guilt.

Here's a way to extend the flavor (and oils) of purchased whipped topping. Blend together 3/4 cup plain nonfat yogurt and 1/3 cup nonfat dry milk powder. Add sugar substitute to equal 2 Tablespoons sugar, 1 cup Cool Whip Lite and 1/2 teaspoon of the flavoring of your choice (vanilla, coconut or almond are all good choices). Gently mix and use as you would whipped topping. The texture is almost a cross between marshmallow cream and whipped cream. This is enough to mound high on a pie.

For turkey gravy with all the "old time" flavor but without the extra fat, here is an almost effortless way to make it. It's almost as easy as opening up a store bought jar. Pour the juice off the turkey. Either place in a large flat bowl and put in the freezer until the fat congeals on top and skim off, or buy one of the new pitchers just made for skimming fat from liquid at your kitchen gadget store. Pour about 2 cups skimmed broth into a medium saucepan. Cook over medium heat. In a covered jar, combine 1/2 cup water or potato broth with 3 tablespoons flour. Mix well. Pour flour mixture into warmed broth. Combine well using a wire whisk. Continue cooking until gravy thickens. Season with salt and pepper to taste.

My Favorite Recipes

Recipe   Page

_____

_____

_____

_____

_____

_____

_____

_____

_____

_____

_____

_____

_____

_____

_____

_____

_____

_____

_____

_____

_____

INDEX

SOUPS

SALADS

VEGETABLES

MAIN DISHES

DESSERTS

THIS AND THAT

FREE RECIPES FREE RECIPES

WELCOME TO THE HEALTHY EXCHANGES FAMILY! I like to feel everyone using my recipes is part of the Family. As you may have purchased this cookbook other than directly from me, I may not even know you are using the recipes.

If you would take the time to drop me a note *with your address* telling me *where* you purchased this cookbook, I will be more than happy to send you a **FREE HEALTHY EXCHANGES DESSERT RECIPE BOOKLET** for your trouble. Please include a business-size, self-addressed stamped envelope. The booklet has 16 recipes we just didn't have room for in this cookbook. But, every one is a winner in it's own right.

Thanks and feel free to call or write me anytime. I think you will enjoy being a part of the Family.

Name_____

Address_____

City _____ State _____ Zip_____

Where Purchased _____

_____

To receive your FREE Recipes, send this form *and*
Self-Addressed, Stamped, Business-Size Envelope to:

HEALTHY EXCHANGES
JoAnna M. Lund
P.O. Box 124
DeWitt, Iowa 52742-0124

ORDER FORM FOR NEWSLETTER

A 12 page monthly newsletter filled with new and exciting low fat, low sugar recipes.

Sold on "Anniversary" basis.

_____Yes, I want to subscribe to the
HEALTHY EXCHANGES NEWSLETTER

$22.00 Yearly Subscription Cost..................................$_____

❏ Sample copy $2.50 each

* *

Please make check payable to HEALTHY EXCHANGES
or order by VISA/MASTERCARD

CARD NUMBER Expiration date_____/____

_____

Required for all credit card orders.   Signature

ORDER TOLL FREE - Visa & Mastercard   1-800-766-8961

Name_____

Address_____

City_____State _____ Zip_____

Telephone (_____) _____

If additional orders are to be sent to an address other than the one listed above, please use a separate sheet and attach to this form.

Mail to: **HEALTHY EXCHANGES**
P.O. Box 124
DeWitt, Iowa 52742-0124
(319) 659-8234

Thank You for your order!

ORDER FORM FOR NEWSLETTER

A 12 page monthly newsletter filled with new and exciting low fat, low sugar recipes.

Sold on "Anniversary" basis.

_____Yes, I want to subscribe to the
    HEALTHY EXCHANGES NEWSLETTER

$22.00 Yearly Subscription Cost.................................$_____

☐ Sample copy $2.50 each

* *

Please make check payable to HEALTHY EXCHANGES
or order by VISA/MASTERCARD

CARD NUMBER   Expiration date_____/____

Required for all credit card orders.   Signature

ORDER TOLL FREE - Visa & Mastercard   1-800-766-8961

Name_____

Address_____

City_____State_____ Zip_____

Telephone (_____) _____

If additional orders are to be sent to an address other than the one listed above, please use a separate sheet and attach to this form.

Mail to: **HEALTHY EXCHANGES**
              P.O. Box 124
              DeWitt, Iowa 52742-0124
              (319) 659-8234

Thank You for your order!